D1313850

Success in Writing

Writing to Tell a Story

GLOBE FEARON
EDUCATIONAL PUBLISHER
A Division of Simon & Schuster
Upper Saddle River, New Jersey

Executive Editor: Barbara Levadi
Senior Editor: Francie Holder
Project Editors: Karen Bernhaut, Douglas Falk, Amy Jolin
Editorial Assistant: Kris Shepos-Salvatore
Editorial Development: Kraft & Kraft
Production Director: Penny Gibson
Production Editor: Alan Dalgleish
Interior Design and Electronic Page Production: Blue Inc.
Marketing Manager: Nancy Surridge
Cover Design: Leslie Baker, Pat Smythe

Copyright © 1996 by Globe Fearon Educational Publisher, a division of Simon and Schuster, One Lake Street, Upper Saddle River, New Jersey, 07458. All rights reserved. No part of this book may be reproduced or transmitted in any form or by any means, electrical or mechanical, including photocopying, recording, or by any information storage and retrieval system, without permission in writing from the publisher.

Printed in the United States of America
3 4 5 6 7 8 9 10   99 98

ISBN 0-835-91889-0

GLOBE FEARON EDUCATIONAL PUBLISHER
A Division of Simon & Schuster
Upper Saddle River, New Jersey

CONTENTS

UNIT 1 Understanding Narration **5**

Chapter 1 Starting with the Basics **6**

   Lesson 1 Beginning a Narrative......................... **8**

   Lesson 2 Building Conflict in the Middle........................ **9**

   Lesson 3 Reaching the End **10**

Chapter 2 Narrating with Style........................... **11**

   Lesson 1 Using Sensory Details **12**

   Lesson 2 Choosing a Narrator and Point of View..................... **13**

   Lesson 3 Putting Events in Order **14**

What Have You Learned in Unit 1? **15**

UNIT 2 Writing to Tell a Story **16**

Chapter 1 Planning Your Writing **17**

   Lesson 1 Choosing a Topic **18**

   Lesson 2 Narrowing a Topic **19**

   Lesson 3 Identifying the Audience **21**

   Lesson 4 Identifying the Purpose **22**

   Lesson 5 Gathering Details **23**

   Lesson 6 Organizing a Sequence of Events **25**

   Lesson 7 Creating a Plot........................ **27**

Chapter 2 Developing Your Writing **29**

   Lesson 1 Drafting the Beginning **30**

   Lesson 2 Drafting the Middle **31**

   Lesson 3 Drafting the Ending **32**

Chapter 3 Completing Your Writing......................... **33**

   Lesson 1 Revising Your Essay **34**

   Lesson 2 Proofreading Your Essay **36**

   Lesson 3 Publishing Your Essay **37**

What Have You Learned in Unit 2? **38**

UNIT 3 Writing on Your Own 39

Chapter 1 Writing a Personal Narrative 40

   Lesson 1 Choosing a Topic 41

   Lesson 2 Gathering Details 42

   Lesson 3 Writing in the First Person 44

   Lesson 4 Writing Your Personal Narrative 45

Chapter 2 Writing an Eyewitness Account 47

   Lesson 1 Selecting Vivid Details 48

   Lesson 2 Organizing by Chronological Order 49

   Lesson 3 Drafting Your Eyewitness Account 51

   Lesson 4 Completing Your Eyewitness Account 52

Chapter 3 Writing a Humorous Anecdote 53

   Lesson 1 Building to the Punch Line 54

   Lesson 2 Making an Anecdote Funny 56

   Lesson 3 Drafting Your Humorous Anecdote 58

   Lesson 4 Completing Your Humorous Anecdote 59

What Have You Learned in Unit 3? 60

UNIT 4 Writing on Assignment 61

Chapter 1 Writing a Test Essay 62

   Lesson 1 Understanding the Prompt 64

   Lesson 2 Organizing Your Thoughts Quickly 65

   Lesson 3 Drafting Under a Deadline 67

   Lesson 4 Completing a Test Essay 68

Chapter 2 Writing a Biographical Account 69

   Lesson 1 Getting Information from an Interview 70

   Lesson 2 Organizing from an Angle 71

   Lesson 3 Writing Your Biographical Account 73

What Have You Learned in Unit 4? 74

The Writing Process 75

A Guide for Writers: Grammar, Mechanics, and Usage .76

UNIT 1 Understanding Narration

Narration, or narrative writing, is writing that tells a story. You tell a story when you answer the question "What happened?" The story can be about something that really happened, or it can be a story that you make up.

What to Do

Use narrative writing to tell the stories that interest you and that you want to share with others. You might use the following kinds of narrative writing:

- A personal narrative tells about an experience from your life and shows its importance.
- An eyewitness account describes an event in such vivid detail that the audience feels they have experienced it.
- A humorous anecdote is a short, entertaining story, usually about a particular event or episode.

How to Do It

Follow these guidelines when you write a narrative:

- Build your story around a plot, or a series of events.
- Focus on a struggle, called a conflict.
- Present interesting characters.
- Have the action take place in a particular time and place, called the setting.
- Have a narrator tell the story from a particular point of view.
- Include a central message, or theme, if you like.

Review It

1. What is the purpose of narrative writing?

_____

_____

2. List two examples of narrative writing.

_____

_____

3. List two guidelines to follow when you write a narrative.

_____

_____

CHAPTER 1 Starting with the Basics

A narrative has a beginning, a middle, and an end. What else does a narrative have? Most often, it has characters, a setting, a plot, and a theme. When you write a narrative about something that really happened, you recreate these elements from your memory of the experience. When you write fiction, you create these elements from your imagination.

What to Do

To begin thinking about the characters, setting, plot, and theme of your narrative, ask yourself, "Who? What? Where? When? How? Why?"

- Characters are the people in your narrative. Each character looks, moves, and talks in his or her own way. A character may also have a trait, such as humor or honesty. A character takes action because of something he or she wants. Most often, a character faces a struggle, called a conflict.
- Setting is the time and place in which your story happens. Vivid details can bring the setting to life and create a mood, or atmosphere.
- Plot is a series of events. Most often, the plot is driven by a conflict between characters or within a character. Sometimes a character struggles against nature.
- Theme is a central message. Some narratives have a theme. When a narrative is based on personal experience, the theme might explain the importance of the writer's experience.

How to Do It

Look for the characters, setting, plot, and theme in the following narrative. It is the first part of a humorous anecdote that a student named Vince wrote.

> After I learned how to make spaghetti with fresh tomato sauce, I invited my grandparents to dinner at our house. I guess I wanted to prove something to myself. I wanted to show myself that I could make a wonderful meal for my family, on my own, without any help.
>
> I spent all day in the kitchen, chopping and cooking tomatoes, garlic, onions, and basil. My mother kept checking on me. Each time, she shook her head and laughed.
>
> "I can't believe you're doing this!" she said. "Your sauce smells delicious!"
>
> Even my older brother Tony, who likes

to give me a hard time, was impressed. More than once he offered to do a taste test.

"Hey, it's perfect," he said. "Don't change a thing!"

Finally, after hours of preparation, dinner was ready. Mom decorated the table with flowers and fancy dinner napkins. Grandpa wore a tie for the occasion. Grandma wore her new blue dress. My brother, as usual, wore his baseball cap.

I served everyone a big portion of spaghetti. Everyone exclaimed their praise—everyone except Grandpa. He was so busy eating, he didn't once look up from his plate! I thought he'd given me the best compliment.

Then, my Grandma said, "Oh, you know Grandpa. He'll eat anything!"

Review It

1. Who are the characters in the anecdote?

_____

_____

2. What is the setting?

_____

_____

3. How did the narrator feel about the event?

_____

_____

4. What was the funny thing that happened?

_____

_____

_____

_____

Lesson 1   Beginning a Narrative

The beginning of your narrative sets the scene, introduces characters, and establishes the conflict of the plot. Because the beginning does so much, you want your first words to grab your readers' attention and keep them reading.

What to Do

Here are a few strategies for beginning your narrative:

- Introduce the narrative's most interesting character.
- Begin with one detail of plot, setting, or character.
- Begin with dialogue.
- Give hints about where the narrative will lead.

How to Do It

Look at this example. It is the beginning of a personal narrative that a student named Jasmine wrote. Jasmine began her narrative by describing the most interesting characters.

> He was a retired plumber named Raymond. On Saturday afternoons, Raymond liked to take the bus to our neighborhood to visit with his old friend Henry. Henry was my great uncle. Both Raymond and Uncle Henry loved baseball. Often, we all watched baseball games on television at Uncle Henry's. Raymond was a Cubs fan, and Henry liked the Mets. True and loyal fans, they knew the name and number of every player. Sometimes they disagreed with the umpire's calls.

Review It

▶ Rewrite Jasmine's beginning. First, take another look at the way she began. She used the first strategy listed in What to Do. Think about the other strategies for writing a beginning. Choose one of those other strategies to rewrite Jasmine's beginning.

1. Underline the strategy you choose.
2. Write your new beginning on the lines below.

_____

_____

_____

_____

_____

Lesson 2 Building Conflict in the Middle

The middle of a narrative tells the events of the story in the order they happened. Each event adds to the conflict. The conflict reaches a high point, or climax. As the characters struggle with the conflict, we learn what they are like.

What to Do

Build the story around the conflict, or struggle. It may be a struggle between two characters. For example, two characters may want the same job. Characters may also struggle against nature, such as trying to escape a hurricane or a fire. They can even struggle within themselves. For example, they may have to decide how to deal with a crisis or a question of honesty.

How to Do It

Look at this example. It is part of the middle of Jasmine's personal narrative about Raymond and Uncle Henry.

> One summer, the three of us watched on television one of the great rival games between the Cubs and the Mets. The teams were tied at the bottom of the ninth inning. The bases were loaded and the Cubs had two outs. Ron Santo, third baseman for the Cubs, was up to bat. That summer, Santo had been in a slump.
>
> "Extra innings! Extra innings! Santo won't know where to find the ball!" my Uncle Henry hooted with delight.
>
> Raymond beamed, "Santo has been saving his strength just for this moment. He's going to hit it out of the park!"
>
> Santo swung and missed. He swung at the next pitch and missed again. Raymond and Uncle Henry glared at each other.
>
> "Strike three coming up," Uncle Henry hollered.
>
> "Let's go, Santo! Hit it out of the park!" shouted Raymond.
>
> Santo stepped into the batter's box. The pitcher wound up for the next throw.

Review It

1. What is the conflict between Raymond and Uncle Henry?

_____

2. How do the events of the ball game add to the conflict between Raymond and Uncle Henry?

_____

_____

Lesson 3   Reaching the End

The end of a narrative brings the action to a close. The end also shows how the conflict is resolved and how the characters are affected.

What to Do

Here are a few ways to end your narrative.

- End with a thought that will stay in your readers' minds.
- End with a quotation.
- End the suspense.
- Solve the conflict.
- Tell about the importance of the event.
- Tell what a character learned from the event.
- Tell what happens to a character years later.

How to Do It

Look at this example. It is the end of the personal narrative written by Jasmine.

> Santo cracked the ball with his bat. Suddenly, we were all on our feet in front of the television.
>
> "There it goes! It's gone! It's a home run!" Raymond shouted.
>
> "I don't believe it!" Uncle Henry cried.
>
> Two outfielders raced to the fence, but the ball had sailed out of the ball park. Santo ran around the bases, tagging each one with his toe. At home plate, a swarm of happy teammates waited to congratulate him.
>
> Uncle Henry, Raymond, and I watched with wide grins on our faces. Seeing a player hit a home run is a thrill, no matter which team the player is on.
>
> "Well, that was a beauty, Raymond. I guess everyone gets lucky sometimes," Uncle Henry said, winking at me.
>
> Raymond smiled. "Yeah, maybe next time it'll be your team."

Review It

1. In What to Do, underline the strategies that Jasmine used to end her personal narrative.
2. How is the suspense of the ball game ended?

_____

3. How is the conflict between Raymond and Uncle Henry resolved?

_____

CHAPTER 2 Narrating with Style

Vivid details, point of view, and chronological order help make your narrative writing clear. Vivid details build memorable characters. First-person point of view creates a believable narrator. Chronological order helps the reader understand the events of the narrative.

What to Do
Use your narrative style to bring a story to life, make it clear, and keep it moving. In this chapter, you will learn three ways to make your style effective:

Using Sensory Details
Choosing a Narrator and Point of View
Putting Events in Order

How to Do It
To make your readers feel that they are in the setting of your story, use vivid sensory details. Sensory details appeal to the readers' five senses.

An icy gust of wind roared through the alley and sent a trash can clattering into the gutter.

Also use vivid details to make your characters interesting and memorable.

Curtis leaned back and looked at the cap he was holding. It was the cap I had given him for his birthday.
"This might bring me luck," he said. "If I believed in luck." He smiled and put the cap on. "It's worth a try," he said.

Use chronological order to help your readers follow the story. If something is out of order, tell them when it happened.

By 1944, both Charlie Parker and Dizzy Gillespie had been playing in jazz groups for about ten years. That year, they met in New York City. The following year, they formed their own group and invented the kind of jazz called bebop.

Apply It
▶ Find examples of different narrative styles. Good places to look include literature anthologies, magazines, books of stories, or novels. Remember that narratives can be about true events or fictional ones. Notice the way the writers have created effective narrative styles. If you can, discuss the examples with a partner or group.

Lesson 1 Using Sensory Details

Sensory details tell what can be seen, heard, felt, tasted, or smelled. In narrative writing, you use sensory details to help your reader experience what you are telling about. Details describe characters and setting. They also let readers feel that they are at the scene of your story.

What to Do Observe, recall, or make up the details that will bring the setting and characters of your narrative to life. Make lists of details that you want the readers to see, hear, feel, taste, or smell. A sensory detail web can help you gather details about your topic. You will see how to use one in Unit 2.

How to Do It Look at this example. It is the beginning of a personal narrative that a student named Darnell wrote. Notice the sensory details.

> I had the most spectacular experience at basketball camp because of one very ordinary encounter. During the two weeks of camp, I practiced basketball skills with a hundred other young players. We ran drills until our shirts were so wet they stuck to our skin. The arena where we practiced smelled like a giant sweat sock. The huge dome of the arena sprouted from the ground like a mushroom. Inside, the arena was as dark as a cave, except for the court, which gleamed. When we weren't playing basketball, we were talking about it. Our eyes sparkled like polished trophies when we whispered the names of the great players: Shaquille O'Neal, Hakeem Olajuwon, Patrick Ewing, and Michael Jordan.

Review It **1.** List one sense-of-sight detail from the narrative.

_____

2. List one sense-of-smell detail from the narrative.

_____

3. Write a sentence to add to the narrative. Use a detail for the sense of hearing.

_____

_____

Lesson 2 Choosing a Narrator and Point of View

When you write a narrative, you need to decide who will be your narrator, the person who tells the story. Your readers will experience the story through your narrator's words. You also need to choose a point of view. The point of view you choose determines how much your audience can learn from the narrator.

What to Do

Choose a point of view for your narrative. Here are a few characteristics of two points of view that you can use.

First-person Point of View
- The narrator tells about events that happened to him or her.
- The narrator uses the pronouns *I*, *me*, and *we*.
- The narrator reveals his or her thoughts and feelings.
- The narrator does not know the thoughts and feelings of other characters.

Third-person Point of View
- The narrator may tell about what happens to many characters.
- The narrator uses third-person pronouns *he*, *she*, and *they*.
- The narrator may know the thoughts and feelings of other characters.

Personal narratives and eyewitness accounts are usually written from the first-person point of view. Accounts from history usually use the third-person.

How to Do It

Look at this example. It is part of an eyewitness account written by a student named Maya. Because her narrative is an eyewitness account, Maya used the first-person point of view.

> My brother José and I leaned our elbows on the ledge of the window. Three stories down, people gathered outside for the street fair. The smell of tortillas drifted up to the window, and my stomach rumbled. Suddenly, a band started playing. People danced on the sidewalk and street. I tapped my fingers on the window ledge. I wanted to dance, too.

Review It

1. Underline the pronouns that Maya uses to refer to herself.
2. Write a new sentence to add to the eyewitness account. Be sure to use the first-person point of view.

_____

3. Rewrite the first sentence from the third-person point of view.

_____

Lesson 3 Putting Events in Order

Chronological order is the order in which events occur in time. This kind of order is often used in narrative writing.

What to Do

It is *usually* best to put the events in the order in which they happened. Sometimes, however, you will want to present them out of order. For example, you may want to explain about something that a character did long ago.

Throughout your narrative, be sure to tell your readers when events take place. Use special words and phrases called *transitional words and phrases* to help readers understand the order of events.

Transitional Words and Phrases		
at first	finally	later
then	after a while	that afternoon
the next day	early in the day	at last
suddenly	later that night	before

How to Do It

Look at this example. It is part of a narrative essay written by a student named Miguel. Note how he orders the events.

> Early that evening, I rode the bus to the concert hall.
> My favorite band, "The Electric Toads," was giving a
> performance that night. At first, it looked as if I might be
> the only fan in the huge, empty hall. After a while, the hall
> filled with fans, and the band leaped onto the stage. Soon,
> all of the fans were dancing in the aisles.

Review It

1. What happens first in Miguel's essay?

_____

2. What happens last?

_____

3. List the transitional words and phrases that Miguel used in his narrative.

_____

_____

What Have You Learned in Unit 1?

Use these questions to gather and review your thoughts about the importance of each of the key points in Unit 1. Don't worry about writing complete sentences. Just put some thoughts, ideas, and reactions down for each question.

1. What is narrative writing?

_____

2. What is one kind of conflict that a character might have?

_____

3. What should you include when you are describing a setting?

_____

4. Why would you give a narrative a plot?

_____

5. Why would you give a narrative a theme?

_____

6. What is one strategy for beginning a narrative?

_____

7. What is one strategy for ending a narrative?

_____

8. Why should you use sensory details in a narrative?

_____

9. Which point of view would you use for a personal narrative?

_____

10. Why should you use transitional words and phrases in a narrative?

_____

▶ If you can, share your answers with a partner or group. Work together to make a list of "Five Great Ways to Tell a Story."

UNIT 2 Writing to Tell a Story

Writing is like walking. You take one step at a time. Writing a narrative essay may seem like more than you can handle when you first think about doing it. If you break it into steps, each step will seem easier.

What to Do

Follow three basic steps as you write to tell a story. In this unit, you will learn the three basic steps.

Planning Your Writing
Developing Your Writing
Completing Your Writing

How to Do It

Keep this outline in mind. It shows the smaller steps within the three large ones.

Plan your writing.
Choose a topic.
Narrow the topic.
Identify the audience.
Identify the purpose.
Gather the information and details you need.
Organize your story.

Develop your writing.
Draft the beginning.
Draft the middle.
Draft the ending.

Complete your writing.
Revise your essay.
Proofread your essay.
Publish your essay.

Apply It

▶ Imagine yourself writing narration. Begin by looking for examples of narrative writing in the everyday world. You may already have examples in your notebook from your work on page 11. If not, look in magazines, collections of stories, and history books. Choose a narrative, and imagine that you were writing it. Visualize yourself going through each step. If you can, discuss the steps with a partner or group.

Plan what you want to say in your narrative. Plan how to say it. You will have a much better chance of telling an interesting story if you do.

What to Do

Get your writing off to a good start. Your writing begins long before you start your first draft. You actually begin writing as soon as you begin thinking about the story you want to tell. Many of your first ideas will appear in the final draft of your writing. Taking the time to think and plan at the start will make that final draft as good as it can be.

How to Do It

Follow this checklist. In this chapter, you will work through all the steps that are needed to plan a narrative essay. They are listed in this checklist.

- ☐ Start by choosing a topic that is important to you. As you think about topics, remember that a narrative essay tells a story. Your essay will be strongest if you collect a few ideas for topics and then choose the best of them. List topics in your notebook.

- ☐ Once you have chosen your topic, narrow it until it fits your assignment and the space and time available to you. Focus on the heart of the story. Ask yourself questions about the story to narrow the topic.

- ☐ Think about the people who will read your finished narrative. Different audiences have different interests and experiences. By knowing who your readers are, you can write in a way that will appeal to them.

- ☐ Decide what your purpose for writing is. The main purpose for writing a narrative essay is to tell a story about something that happened. You also need to decide how you want the story to affect your readers.

- ☐ Gather information about the events in your story, and gather sensory details to bring these events to life.

- ☐ Organize your story so that your readers will understand it and find it interesting. Use chronological order to present events in the order that they happened.

Apply It

▶ As you complete the lessons in this chapter, return to this page to check off each step. You will be able to see the progress you are making.

Lesson 1 Choosing a Topic

Have you ever seen a wildfire, an ice storm, or a flood? Have you ever gone to a basketball game? How about a baseball game? What happened? Use your observation skills to look closely at everything around you. Then you'll always have a supply of good topics for narrative essays.

What to Do

A narrative essay tells a story. To come up with topics for your essay, make a list of experiences. A personal events time line will get your memory flowing.

How to Do It

Look at the events that a student named Jamal listed. He put a check mark next to the topic he liked best.

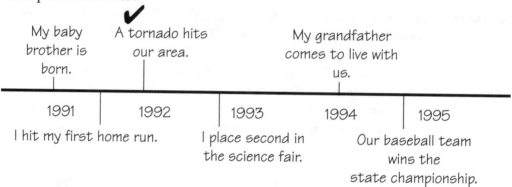

Apply It

▶ Make your own time line on a separate sheet of paper. You may find it easier to work *backwards*. Start with the present and go back in time. Include about 5 to 10 experiences.

▶ Some experiences make better narrative essay topics than others. To help you choose your topic, answer these questions about your time line.

1. Which experience is most important to you?

_____

2. Which experience can you remember most clearly?

_____

3. Which experience will be most meaningful for your readers?

_____

4. Based on your answers to these questions, which experience will you write about?

_____

Lesson 2 Narrowing a Topic

Once you have chosen your topic, narrow it until it fits your assignment and the space and time available to you. Narrowing your topic means deciding what part of a subject you want to explore in a piece of writing.

What to Do Focus on one event. Suppose you have been assigned to write an essay of three paragraphs. The topic "The Tornado of 1992," is too large, or broad. You wouldn't be able to cover it in just three paragraphs. You might narrow it down to "My Experience with a Tornado." That topic could be handled well in three paragraphs.

How to Do It Use a topic web to explore your topic. Look at Jamal's topic web. First, he wrote his topic in the central oval. Then, in each oval connected to it, he jotted down an idea about his topic. He saw that all four ideas would not fit in his essay. He focused on one of them. He chose to write about his experience of actually seeing a tornado. He narrowed his topic to "My Experience with a Tornado."

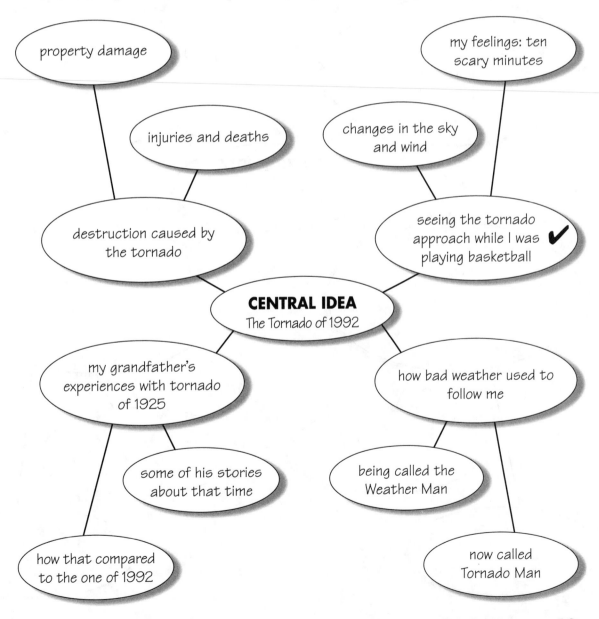

Apply It ▶ Use this web to narrow your topic. Write your topic in the central oval. Write an idea about the topic in each of the ovals connected to it. In the smaller ovals add details about each of these ideas. Then decide which idea you feel most strongly about. Choose that one to develop. Adjust your topic to match the choice you have made.

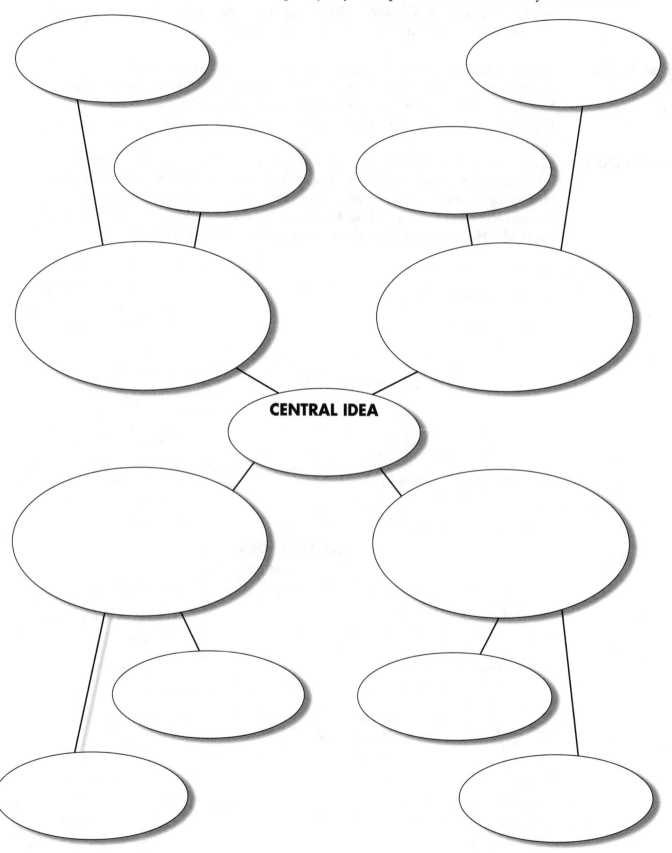

CENTRAL IDEA

Lesson 3 Identifying the Audience

Your audience is the group of people who will read or listen to your narrative essay. Different audiences have different interests and experiences. They also have different levels of knowledge.

What to Do

Think about who your readers are. Decide what they know about your topic and what they are interested in finding out about it. Then you can write in a way that will appeal to them.

How to Do It

Look at this example. It is part of Jamal's narrative essay about seeing a tornado. His audience is his social studies teacher and classmates. In the first paragraph, Jamal focuses on his classmates. In the second paragraph, he focuses on his social studies teacher.

Jamal helps his friends put themselves in the scene and understand his feelings by including details about shooting baskets.

> At first, I thought a thunderstorm was brewing. Dark clouds rumbled and raced across the sky. As the wind picked up, big oak trees swayed like slow dancers. I figured I had time before the storm hit to shoot a few more baskets. I dribbled the ball down the court and aimed for the basket. Then, on the rebound, I happened to look up at the sky again. The color of the sky had changed from yellow to green. In the distance, I saw a black funnel approaching.
>
> I realized that I was seeing a tornado. Suddenly, I remembered all of my grandfather's stories about the Great Tornado of 1925. It swept across three states, snapped off trees, destroyed houses, and killed nearly 700 people.

To appeal to his social studies teacher, Jamal includes details about the impact of another tornado.

Apply It

▶ Answer the following questions to help identify the audience for your essay.

1. Who will read or listen to your narrative essay?

_____

2. What does your audience need or want to know about your topic?

_____

_____

_____

_____

Lesson 4   Identifying the Purpose

You already know that the main purpose for writing a narrative essay is to tell a story about something that happened. You need to identify another purpose as well. You need to decide how you want your readers to feel when they read your essay.

What to Do   Decide what emotions you want your readers to feel while they're reading your essay. Do you want them to laugh? Do you want them to feel tense or scared?

How to Do It   Look at this example. It is another passage that Jamal wrote about seeing the tornado. As you read it, think about how he wanted his audience to feel.

> Sweat trickled down my face as I jumped for the ball. I was the only kid playing on the steaming basketball court. It really was too hot to play, but suddenly, a cool breeze whipped across the court. It was so cold that I shivered. It grew stronger and stronger until it swept across the court and swayed the treetops. Dark clouds dimmed the sunlight. Thunder crashed in the sky. Then, all was quiet. The only sound I heard was the bounce of the basketball on the concrete court. Something was about to happen.

Review It   **1.** How did you feel while reading this passage?

_____

2. List three details that Jamal used to create that feeling.

_____

_____

_____

Apply It   ▶ What is the purpose for your narrative essay? To identify your purpose, ask yourself how you want your readers to feel while they're reading your essay. State this purpose in a sentence.

_____

_____

Lesson 5 Gathering Details

To develop a narrative essay, include two kinds of details. First, include details that describe events. Second, add sensory details to help your readers experience the events.

What to Do

To gather details about events, ask yourself *who, what, when, where, why,* and *how* questions. Then use a sensory details web to recall or invent sensory details.

How to Do It

Look at these examples. First, look at the questions and answers that Jamal used to gather details about events.

WHO was involved in the event?	myself, alone
WHAT was the event ?	a tornado
WHEN did the event take place?	One hot, humid afternoon in the summer of 1992
WHERE did the event take place?	at the basketball courts
WHY did the event take place?	weather like a thunderstorm
HOW did the event take place?	rushing suddenly down on me, in the shape of a huge black funnel

Second, look at the web Jamal created to gather sensory details for his narrative essay.

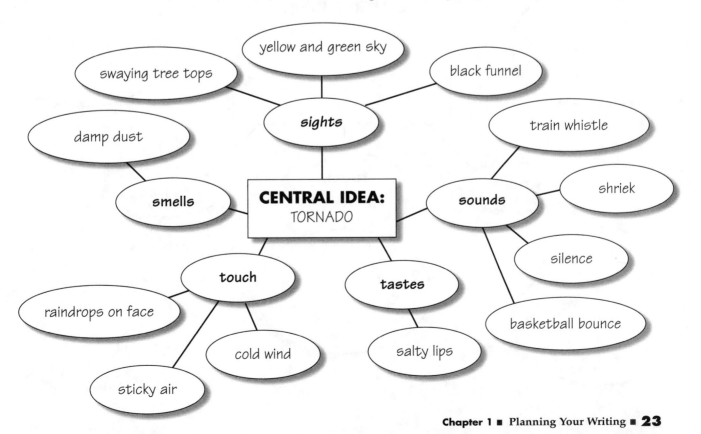

Apply It

▶ Gather the basic information and details you will need for your narrative.

▶ First, ask yourself *who, what, when, where, why,* and *how* questions about your topic. Write your answers on a separate sheet of paper.

▶ Then use this sensory details web to gather the vivid details that will bring the events in your narrative to life. Add more ovals if you need them.

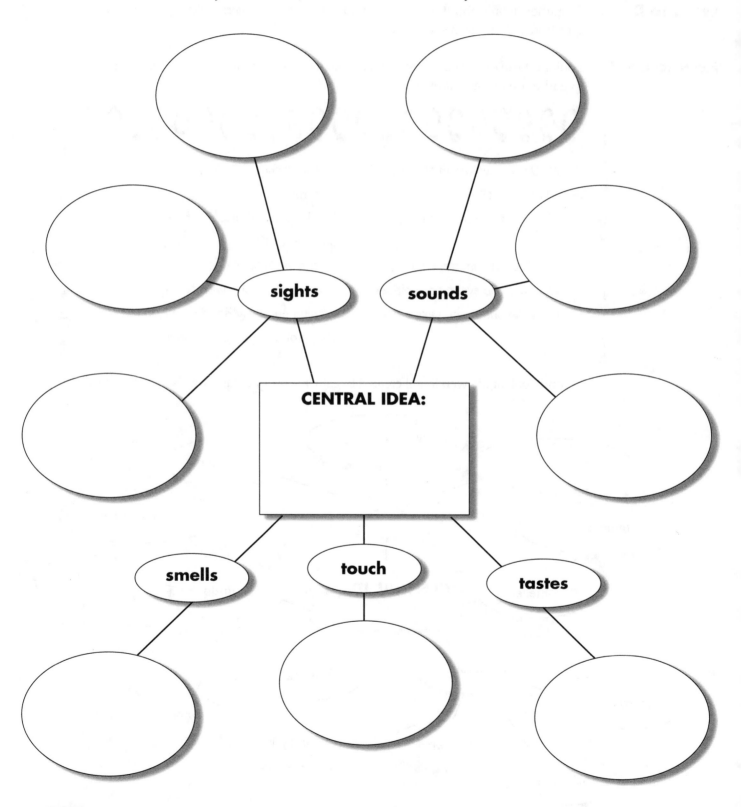

Lesson 6   Organizing a Sequence of Events

In a narrative essay, the best way to present the events is in the order of time. This is called chronological order. If you are writing about something that actually happened, it is usually best to organize events in the order in which they occurred.

What to Do   Use a sequence of events to organize a true account. An event map can help you organize the events.

How to Do It   Look at the event map that Jamal used to organize the events of the tornado story.

Event Map

Topic: My eyewitness account of watching a tornado

Central Idea: While I was playing basketball one hot afternoon, a storm developed into a tornado.

Event 1: A thunderstorm brewed. The temperature dropped, the wind picked up, and a few raindrops fell. The sky turned yellow, then green.

Event 2: I saw a black funnel cloud in the distance. The tornado headed toward our town and toward the playground. All of a sudden, the birds stopped chirping and the trees stopped swaying. Everything was silent.

Event 3: The silence was broken by what sounded like a train whistle that soon became a wild shriek. The sound of the shriek bolted me into action. I ran like crazy for cover in a ditch.

Conclusion: The tornado lost energy and eventually dragged itself away. As soon as it was safe, I ran for home. At home, I found my family sheltered in the basement. They tried to tell me about the excitement I missed!

Apply It   ▶ Make your own event map. First, on a separate sheet of paper, list the main events that you want to include in your essay. Then enter them on this event map to organize the events in the order they happened.

EVENT MAP

Topic:

Central Idea:

Event 1:

Event 2:

Event 3:

Conclusion:

Lesson 7 Creating a Plot

If you are writing a fictional story, or if you want to give a true story more drama, you can build suspense by creating a plot. There is an important difference between a sequence of events and a plot. A sequence of events simply tells what happened next. A plot is a sequence of events with a shape. The writer may tell events out of order and emphasize some more than others. A plot can build suspense and keep readers interested and excited.

What to Do

Base your plot on a conflict, or struggle, that a character faces. Include rising action, a climax, and a resolution.

- *Conflict* is a struggle between opposing forces or characters. Choose one of the following kinds of conflict for your narrative essay.
    - Two characters come into conflict.
    - A character comes into conflict with an opposing force, such as nature.
    - A conflict arises between a character and a social group.
    - Conflict happens within a character.
- *Rising action* is a pattern of events that adds to the conflict and builds toward the climax. Use events that build the emotion of your narrative.
- The *climax* is the high point of a narrative. Use the most dramatic event in your story as the climax.
- The *resolution* brings a narrative essay to its close. Use an event that winds down your narrative and explains how everything turned out.

How to Do It

Use a plot profile to help you build a plot from the events in your story. Jamal decided to give his essay more drama, so he made this plot profile.

CLIMAX: The high point of the story occurs when I run for a ditch in the playground.

RISING ACTION: The conflict builds when the weather conditions swiftly change, and I see a black funnel cloud.

CONFLICT: I face a conflict against nature. A terrible storm suddenly forms while I am outside playing basketball.

RESOLUTION: The conflict is resolved when the tornado weakens as it travels away. I return home to find my family hiding in the basement.

Apply It   ▶ Chart a plot profile like Jamal's for your narrative essay. Make changes on the profile until you are happy with your plot.

RISING ACTION:

CLIMAX:

CONFLICT:

RESOLUTION:

CHAPTER 2 Developing Your Writing

As you write your drafts, work from your plan. Keep your audience and purpose in mind. Write freely, without trying to make everything perfect. You will improve your drafts later.

What to Do

Get your ideas on paper.

Each version of your writing is called a draft. To get the first draft on paper, start writing wherever it is easiest for you to begin. Maybe you will want to copy a sentence from your notes. Do not worry about spelling or grammar right now. Just get your ideas down on paper.

How to Do It

Follow this checklist. In this chapter, you will work through all the steps that are needed to develop a narrative essay. They are listed in this checklist.

☐ Draft the beginning of your story. Make the beginning grab your readers' attention. You might begin with a vivid description, dialogue between two characters, a surprising statement, or a question. Introduce the characters. Set the scene. Establish the conflict, if there is one.

☐ Draft the middle. You introduced your characters and got the action started in the beginning. Now develop the characters and move the action along in the middle. If your story has a plot, make the action rise to the climax. End the middle of your narrative with the climax itself. Use transitional words to show the sequence of events.

☐ Draft the ending. This is the time to bring the story to a strong finish. There are many ways to end a story. You can explain how the conflict was resolved. You can tie up any loose ends or explain the importance of what took place. You can tell what the characters learned from the events in the story. You can even look ahead to tell what happens to a character years later.

Apply It

▶ As you complete the lessons in this chapter, return to this page to check off each step. You will be able to see the progress you are making.

Lesson 1 Drafting the Beginning

Use the beginning of your narrative to lure readers into your story. Catch their interest and make them want to read on.

What to Do

To grab your readers' attention, open your story in one of the following ways:
- Open with a vivid description. Use a sensory detail web to think of precise nouns, adjectives, and action verbs.
- Open with dialogue between two characters.
- Open with a surprising statement.
- Open with a question.

Include the following key elements in the beginning of your narrative:
- Set the scene. Give details about the setting. Help your readers feel that they are there.
- Introduce the most important characters.
- If your story has a plot, establish the conflict. Let your readers see what struggle will drive your plot.

How to Do It

Look at this example. It is Jamal's draft of his beginning.

The first sentence stirs readers' curiosity by hinting that even though the day seemed normal, it wasn't.

> At first, the day seemed like any normal summer day. I was shooting baskets at the playground. I was the only kid there, since it really was too hot to play. Sweat trickled down my face as I jumped for the ball. Suddenly, a breeze whipped across the steaming court. The air was so cold that I shivered. Dark clouds rumbled across the sky. After that, things happened quickly, and the day turned out to be anything but normal.

The last sentence helps create suspense and leads readers into the rest of the story. They will want to find out *why* and *how* the day turned out to be "anything but normal."

Review It

1. Underline a sentence in Jamal's draft that appeals to the sense of sight.
2. Underline three precise action verbs that Jamal used.
3. Jamal wrote "it really was too hot to play." What is a more precise adjective that Jamal could have used instead of *hot*?

Apply It

▶ On a separate sheet of paper, write a draft of the beginning of your narrative essay. Use your event map from page 26 or plot profile from page 28 to help you get started. Use your sensory detail web from page 24 as a source of vivid details.

Lesson 2   Drafting the Middle

The middle of a narrative is where the action takes place. Keep your story moving and take your readers along with you.

What to Do

Review the events on your event map (page 26) or plot profile (page 28). Write one paragraph for each of the events you described. Use transitional words and phrases to show the sequence of events. Transitional words and phrases for narratives tell when events happened.

Some Transitional Words and Phrases		
First of all	Next	Later
Suddenly	Then	Finally
The next day	Afterward	Earlier that day

How to Do It

Look at this example. In the middle of his essay, Jamal used transitional words to show the sequence of events.

> Suddenly, raindrops fell on my face, but I still wanted to shoot a few more baskets. I dribbled the ball down the court and aimed for the basket. On the rebound, I looked up again at the sky. It was turning yellow. Then it turned green. I thought, "Here comes the storm."
>
> All at once, the wind gathered speed. The huge oak trees at the edge of the park waved their branches as if they were afraid. Birds cried out in alarm. The dark clouds grew larger, racing and swirling around each other. Suddenly, the birds stopped calling. The trees stopped swaying. Everything became silent. The only moving thing was a black funnel cloud, coming my way.

Review It

1. What happens first in this part of Jamal's essay?

_____

2. What happens second in this part of Jamal's essay?

_____

3. Underline three transitional words or phrases that Jamal used.

Apply It

▶ On a separate sheet of paper, write a complete draft of the middle of your narrative essay. Remember to use your detail web and your plot profile or event map to help you.

Lesson 3 Drafting the Ending

Give your essay a strong finish. The ending of a story is like the punch line of a joke. It is what the rest of the story has been building up to. It is the payoff for the readers.

What to Do

Choose one of the following ways to end your narrative essay.
- End with a thought that will stay in your readers' minds.
- End with a quotation.
- End the suspense, resolve the conflict, and tie up any loose ends.
- Explain the importance of the events to the characters in the story.
- Tell what a character learned from the events in the story.
- Tell what happens to a character years later.

How to Do It

Look at this example. In his ending, Jamal decided to end the suspense, resolve the conflict, and tie up the loose ends.

> After a while, the tornado moved on, and its energy dwindled. I remained where I was, flattened in the ditch, until I heard birds chirping. When I tried to stand, my legs felt like rubber bands . All I wanted to do was get back home, so I ran and ran until I arrived there. I found my parents and little brother down in the basement, sheltered against a far wall. We all hugged and talked at once.
>
> My mother said, "It was so exciting! You missed the tornado!"
>
> I laughed and said, "If only you knew!"

Review It

1. The conflict was Jamal against the tornado. How was it resolved?

_____

2. The suspense came from the readers' wondering whether Jamal would be hurt by the tornado. When does the suspense end?

_____

Apply It

▶ Write the draft of the ending of your essay on a separate sheet of paper. Use your detail web and your plot profile or event map to help you.

CHAPTER 3 Completing Your Writing

When the first draft of your narrative essay is written, revise it to make it stronger. Then proofread it to make it correct. Finally, publish it to bring it to your audience.

What to Do

Make your writing better with every draft. Revise the first draft to make a second draft that is better.

Keep working at your drafts until your writing says just what you want it to say as well as you can say it. Draft, revise, and revise again until you are pleased with your work.

How to Do It

Follow this checklist. In this chapter, you will work through all the steps that are needed to complete a narrative essay. They are listed in this checklist.

☐ Revise your essay. Now that you have your story down on paper, it is time to go back and revise. When you revise, you make changes to make sure that you have told your story clearly. Read your draft carefully. Use the revision checklist on page 35 to correct and strengthen your writing.

☐ Proofread your essay. Fix any mistakes in spelling, grammar, and punctuation. Read your revised draft sentence by sentence and word by word, looking for the little mistakes that you might have missed or ignored earlier. Use the proofreading checklist on page 36 to find and correct any mistakes.

☐ Publish your essay to bring it to your audience. Find the best way to reach your audience. Follow the requirements of the publishing method you choose.

Apply It

▶ As you complete the lessons in this chapter, return to this page to check off each step. You will be able to see the progress you are making.

Lesson 1   Revising Your Essay

Revising means changing your work to make it even better. A good way to find out what parts of your essay need improving is to ask a friend to read your essay.

What to Do   Make improvements in your work. Start by reading what you have written. Don't make changes now. Just read.

Then read your work again. This time, begin making changes. Use the revision checklist on the next page to guide your work. Keep making changes until your writing says just what you want to say as well as you can say it. Above all, make sure that you have told your story in a clear way that your reader will be able to follow.

How to Do It   Look at this example. Jamal used the revision checklist as he revised his draft. Here is a portion of his revised essay, showing some of the changes he made.

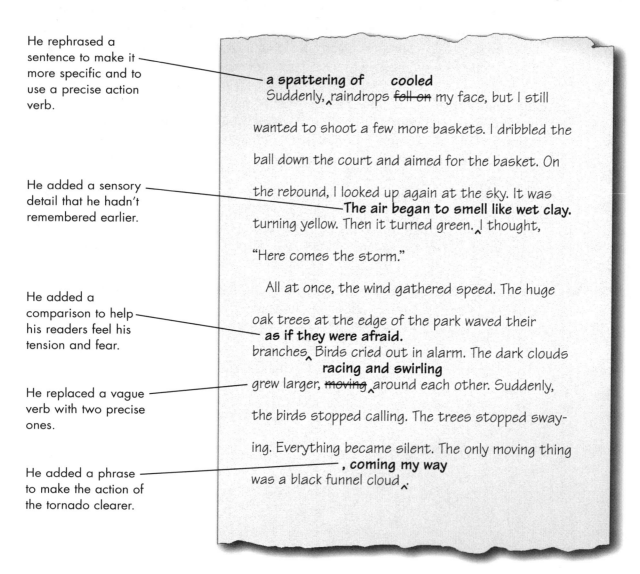

He rephrased a sentence to make it more specific and to use a precise action verb.

a spattering of   cooled
Suddenly, ˄raindrops ~~fell on~~ my face, but I still

wanted to shoot a few more baskets. I dribbled the

ball down the court and aimed for the basket. On

the rebound, I looked up again at the sky. It was
The air began to smell like wet clay.
turning yellow. Then it turned green.˄I thought,

"Here comes the storm."

He added a sensory detail that he hadn't remembered earlier.

    All at once, the wind gathered speed. The huge

oak trees at the edge of the park waved their
 as if they were afraid.
branches˄Birds cried out in alarm. The dark clouds
       racing and swirling
grew larger, ~~moving~~˄around each other. Suddenly,

the birds stopped calling. The trees stopped sway-

ing. Everything became silent. The only moving thing
         , coming my way
was a black funnel cloud ˄.

He added a comparison to help his readers feel his tension and fear.

He replaced a vague verb with two precise ones.

He added a phrase to make the action of the tornado clearer.

Apply It

▶ Use this revision checklist to guide you as you revise your work.

Beginning:
- ☐ Open with a sentence that will lure your readers into your story. If you did not, add a sentence now. If you did, make sure that it grabs the reader's attention.
- ☐ Introduce the most important characters. If you have not, add the sentences that you need now. If you have, try to make the characters more interesting.
- ☐ Describe the setting with vivid sensory details. If you have not, add some details now. If you have, try to use more specific nouns and adjectives.
- ☐ Get the action started. If you have not, add a sentence now. If you have, try to use more specific action verbs.
- ☐ If your story has a plot, establish the conflict. If you have not established the conflict, add a sentence now. If you have, be sure that the reader will understand the struggle.

Middle:
- ☐ Tell the events of the story in chronological order. If they are out of order, rearrange them now.
- ☐ Put each major event in a paragraph of its own. If there are too many events in some paragraphs, divide the middle into more paragraphs.
- ☐ Use transitional words and phrases to help the reader follow the story from one event to the next. If transitions are missing, add them now.
- ☐ If your story has a plot, make the action rise toward the climax. If it does not seem to do that, use more vivid verbs as you get closer to the climax.

End:
- ☐ Bring the action to a conclusion. If you did not include a sentence that shows the reader that the action is over, add one now.
- ☐ Tell the reader how the situation turned out. If you did not do so, add a sentence now.
- ☐ If your story has a plot, tell how the conflict was resolved. If you did not resolve the conflict, add a sentence now.

General:
- ☐ Do not use bland words, such as *great, good,* or *nice.* Replace them with stronger, more specific words.
- ☐ Do not leave grammatical errors in your essay. Correct any that you find. You will take a closer look when you proofread.

▶ If you can, work with a partner to revise your work. Read each other's drafts. Use the revision checklist to find places that might be improved. Make helpful suggestions to improve each other's work.

▶ Think about your partner's suggestions for your essay. Make the final decisions yourself about what to change.

Lesson 2 Proofreading Your Essay

Proofreading is the process of finding and correcting errors in grammar, usage, and mechanics. Follow these steps for proofreading your essay.

What to Do

When you proofread, look for the little mistakes that you might have missed or ignored earlier.

When you are writing a draft, it is a good idea not to worry about grammar and spelling. When you are revising, you should focus on the meaning rather than most mistakes in grammar. *Now* it is time to look for those mistakes. Read your work sentence by sentence and word by word. Use the proofreading checklist below to find and correct any mistakes.

How to Do It

Use the following checklist. It lists problems you may find in narrative writing. You also will find a guide to grammar, usage, and mechanics on pages 76–80.

☐ Make subjects agree with their verbs in number. (Singular subjects need singular verbs. Plural subjects need plural verbs.)

☐ Use complete sentences. Correct any fragments. Correct any run-on sentences.

☐ Use pronouns correctly. Is it clear what noun each pronoun refers to?

☐ Use adjectives to modify nouns or pronouns. Use adverbs to modify verbs, adjectives, and other adverbs.

☐ End each sentence with a period, question mark, or exclamation point.

☐ Use apostrophes correctly in all contractions to show where letters have been taken out.

☐ Use apostrophes correctly to show possession.

☐ Punctuate dialogue correctly:

☐ Use quotation marks to show where a person's exact words begin and end.

☐ Use a comma after words that introduce a quotation: Jamal said, "I had never seen the sky turn green before."

☐ Use a comma after the quotation, inside the quotation marks, when an explanation follows a quotation: "I had never seen the sky turn green before," Jamal said.

☐ Place periods, question marks, and exclamation points inside quotation marks: Jamal said, "I hope I never see the sky turn green again!"

☐ Begin a new paragraph for each new speaker.

☐ Check the essay for spelling errors. If you are unsure about the spelling of certain words, use a dictionary.

Apply It

▶ Use the proofreading checklist to find errors in your work. Correct them. If you can, work with a partner. A fresh eye may see errors that you missed.

Lesson 3 Publishing Your Essay

You have worked hard to prepare your essay and make it as good as you can make it. Now take it to your audience!

What to Do   Find the best way to reach your audience.

How will you publish your narrative? How can you be sure that your audience will see it or hear it? If you can, discuss ideas with a group of students. Consider everyone's suggestions, and then choose the plan that you think is right.

How to Do It   Choose a way of publishing that suits your audience. Here are some suggestions.

Audience	Ways to Publish
Students or adults at school	■ Send your narrative essay to the school literary magazine. ■ Read your essay to your class. ■ With your classmates, put together a collection of your essays to keep in the classroom.
Audiences outside school	■ Submit your narrative essay to a magazine. ■ Enter your narrative essay in a writing contest. ■ Post your narrative essay on an on-line bulletin board. ■ Duplicate copies for family and friends.

Review It   ▶ A strong title will attract readers' attention and make them want to read the essay. Jamal thought of the following three possible titles for his essay:

"The Black Funnel"
"What Can Happen on a Hot Afternoon"
"What Happened the Day the Sky Turned Yellow"

▶ Underline the title that you like best.

Apply It   ▶ Make a clean final copy of your narrative essay. Brainstorm a list of possible titles for your essay. Choose one. Then select one of the choices for publishing your essay.

What Have You Learned in Unit 2?

Use these questions to gather and review your thoughts about the importance of each of the key points in Unit 2. Don't worry about writing complete sentences. Just put some thoughts, ideas, and reactions down for each question.

1. Write one good topic for a three-to-five-paragraph essay.

_____

2. Why is it a good topic?

_____

3. What two kinds of details do you need in a narrative?

_____

4. What should you put in the beginning of a narrative essay?

_____

5. What should you put in the middle of a narrative essay?

_____

6. What should you put in the end of a narrative essay?

_____

7. What do you do when you revise?

_____

8. What do you do when you proofread?

_____

9. What did you enjoy most about writing your narrative essay?

_____

10. What can you do next time to make the writing easier and more enjoyable?

_____

▶ If you can, share your answers with a partner or group. Share the ideas and experiences you had. Since writing is always filled with unexpected twists and turns, talk about what was funny or strange about the experience, too. Come up with a group list called "Tips for Writing Narrative Essays."

UNIT 3 Writing on Your Own

There are many types of narrative writing. You may be familiar with some, such as stories and biographies. They have different forms, but their goals are similar. They are written to tell a story.

What to Do

Become familiar with the three different kinds of narration that you will write in this unit:

A Personal Narrative
An Eyewitness Account
A Humorous Anecdote

How to Do It

Learn the key elements of each kind of narration that you will write.

A personal narrative is your own story. It presents an event from your life and tells why the event was important to you. It has the same elements as a fictional story—characters, setting, and plot. Details bring the people, places, and events to life for your readers.

An eyewitness account recreates an event that the writer has observed. The writer uses details to make the audience feel as if they have experienced it, too. It presents facts, and it usually has an ending that tells about the importance of the event.

A humorous anecdote is a short, entertaining story. Often it is about real people. The purpose of a humorous anecdote is to make the readers laugh. It usually uses dialogue. It may make a point about the way people behave or reveal a personality trait of one of the characters.

Review It

▶ Find examples of each of the types of narration you will write in this unit.

▶ Look for personal narratives in magazines. Look for eyewitness accounts in magazines, in newspapers, and on television. Look for humorous anecdotes in magazines and in book collections of humorous stories. Save the examples in your notebook.

CHAPTER 1 Writing a Personal Narrative

You tell your own story when you write a personal narrative. It is a narrative about you—the writer. It presents an event from your life and tells why the event is important to you.

What to Do

Learn what is unique about a personal narrative. A personal narrative has the same elements as a story—characters, setting, and plot. Details bring the people, places, and events to life for your readers.

How to Do It

Look at this example. It is a personal narrative that a student named Rosa wrote. Rosa's narrative has three parts—a beginning, a middle, and an end.

BEGINNING
Rosa introduced the people, places, and events in her narrative.
She described the setting.
She got the action started.

MIDDLE
She told the events in a clear order.
She used transitional words to make the time clear.

END
She told the readers what the experience meant to her.

> My best friend, Maria, calls me New Shoes. She always has. We met a couple of years ago, on the first day of seventh grade. I was a new student, and I did not know anyone. I stood against the scratchy brick wall, watching the other kids play basketball. I felt lonely and wanted to go home.
>
> Then, while I was staring down at the laces of my new sneakers, someone called out, "Hey, New Shoes!" I looked up and saw a girl with long braids and red ribbons walking toward me. She smiled and said, "Hi, New Shoes. I'm Maria. Do you know how to play guard?"
>
> After we had been friends for a while, Maria told me that she knew how lonely it felt to be the new kid at school. She had been a new student the year before me. Maria and I are still best friends, and she still calls me New Shoes.

Review It

1. Circle the names of the people in the narrative.
2. Underline details that are used to describe Maria.
3. Underline the sentence that tells where Rosa's narrative takes place.
4. Why is Maria's friendship important to Rosa?

_____

_____

_____

Lesson 1   Choosing a Topic

Have you ever made a discovery about yourself? Have you ever experienced an event that was meaningful to you? These kinds of experiences make great topics for personal narratives.

What to Do   Think about times when your life has changed. These are likely to be the times when meaningful events have happened to you.

How to Do It   Use an idea branch to brainstorm topics.

Apply It   ▶ Here is an idea branch of the kinds of events that make good topics for personal narratives. Brainstorm ideas for each branch. Then choose the idea that appeals to you most.

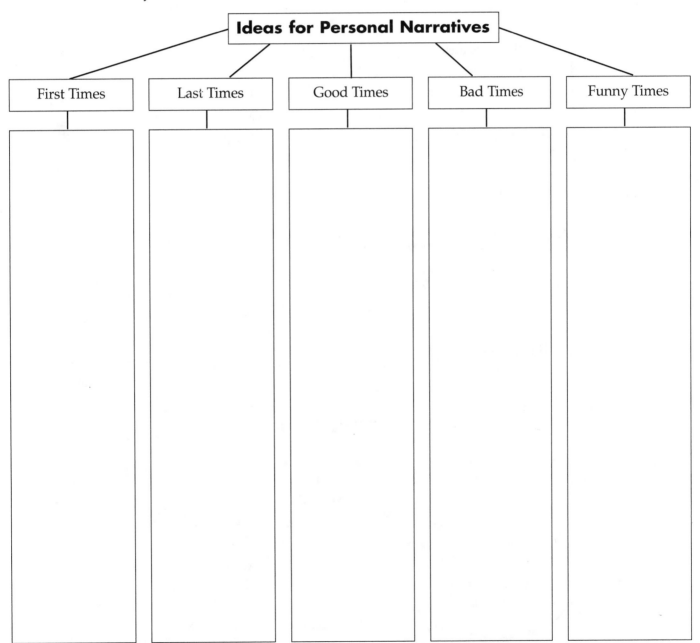

Ideas for Personal Narratives

First Times	Last Times	Good Times	Bad Times	Funny Times

Lesson 2 Gathering Details

Once you have chosen the topic of your personal narrative, gather details. You will need details about events and details that appeal to the five senses. Because the narrative is about your experience, the details should show your feelings.

What to Do

To gather details about events, ask yourself *who, what, when, where, why,* and *how* questions. Then use a sensory details web to come up with vivid details.

How to Do It

Look at these examples. First, look at the questions and answers that Rosa used to gather details about events.

WHO was involved in the event?   Maria and me ("New Shoes")

WHAT was the event?   making friends

WHEN did the event take place?   the first day of school in seventh grade

WHERE did the event take place?   at the playground

WHY did the event take place?   new kid at the school, lonely, Maria's understanding of how that felt

HOW did the event take place?   inviting me to play basketball with the others, giving me a nickname

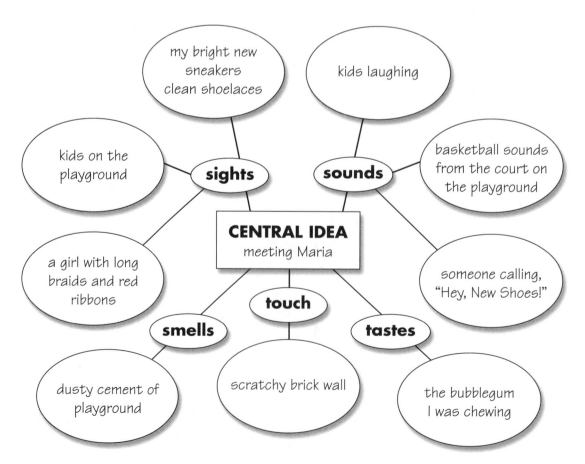

Apply It

▶ Gather the basic information and details you will need for your personal narrative.

▶ First, ask yourself *who, what, when, where, why,* and *how* questions about your topic. Write your answers on a separate sheet of paper.

▶ Then use this sensory details web to gather the vivid details that will bring the events in your narrative to life. Add more ovals if you need them.

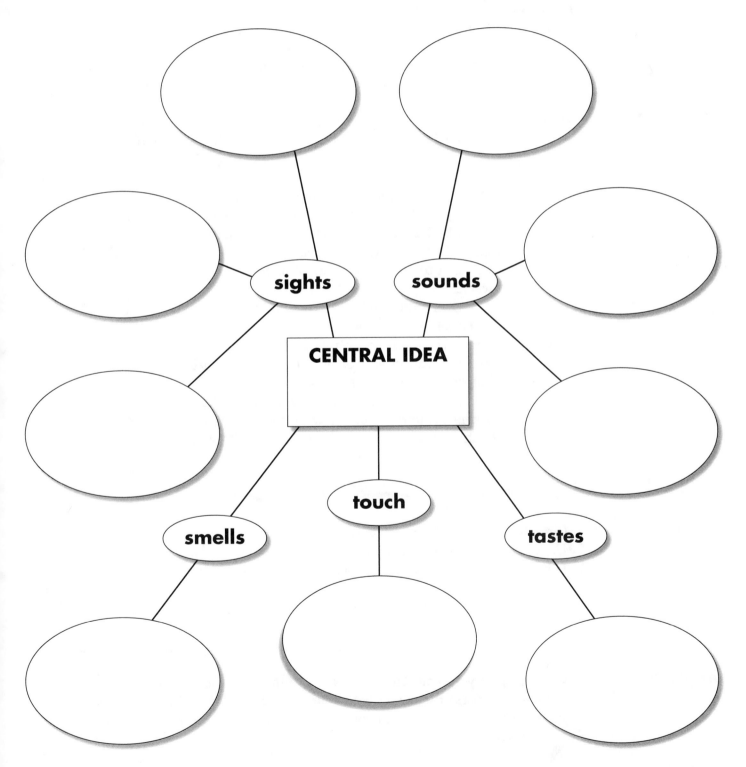

Lesson 3 Writing in the First Person

A first-person narrator tells about events that happened to him or her. In a personal narrative, you are writing about an event that happened to you. Because of that, a personal narrative usually uses the first-person point of view.

What to Do

Recall the characteristics of the first-person point of view.

First-person Point of View
- The narrator tells about events that happened to him or her.
- The narrator uses the pronouns *I*, *me*, and *we*.
- The narrator reveals his or her thoughts and feelings.
- The narrator does not know the thoughts and feelings of other characters.

How to Do It

Look at this example. It is another part of Rosa's personal narrative. Notice that she used first-person point of view to tell about her friendship with Maria.

> Over the years, Maria and I have shared some good times, some funny times, and some bad times. We shared one of our worst times last year, when Maria was so sick that she had to stay in the hospital for two weeks.
>
> Every day while she was in the hospital, I visited her after school. Maria's parents hoped that I could help boost her spirits, so I told her funny stories. Telling these stories helped to boost my spirits, too.
>
> During her hospital stay, I missed having Maria around. I missed walking to school with her and sharing experiences with her.

Review It

1. Circle the pronouns Rosa used to refer to herself.
2. Underline the pronouns Rosa used to refer to Maria.
3. How did Rosa feel about this experience?

_____

_____

Apply It

▶ Begin changing your notes from page 43 into first-person statements. Rewrite your notes as phrases or sentences with yourself as the narrator. Use first-person pronouns to refer to yourself. Add your feelings about each experience that had an effect on you.

You are off to a good start! Now you are ready to write your personal narrative.

Use your notes from pages 43 and 44 to write the draft of your narrative. Use the checklist on the next page to help you revise and proofread it.

How to Do It Look at this example. It is Rosa's draft. Notice how she revised and proofread to make improvements and fix mistakes.

She changed a word to make it more personal.

She rewrote part of a sentence to make it more specific.

She changed a verb to make it closer to her meaning.

She cut a sentence that wasn't related to the idea of funny stories.

She changed verbs to make them more accurate.

She cut words that seemed too exaggerated.

She cut a word that she didn't need.

> Over the years, Maria and I have shared some
>
> good times, funny times, and some bad times.
>
>   our
> We shared one of ~~the~~ worst times last year, when
>   so   that she had to stay   for two weeks
> Maria was ^ ~~really~~ sick ^ in the hospital ^.
>
> Every day while she was in the hospital,
>
> I visited her after school. Maria's parents
> **hoped that**
> ~~thought~~ I could help boost her spirits, so I told
>
> her funny stories. I ~~teased her about not having~~
>
> ~~to take the math test.~~ Telling those stories helped
>
> to boost my spirits, too.
>
>   During her hospital stay, I missed having Maria
>   **walking**
> around. I missed ~~going~~ to school with her. I missed
>   **sharing**
> ~~having~~ experiences with her. One afternoon while
>
> I was visiting, Maria sat up in bed and said, "Hi!"
> **She**
> ~~Suddenly, my dear friend~~ had recovered! I hugged her
>
> and ~~then~~ rushed to the cafeteria to find her parents.

Review It ▶ What other changes could Rosa have made to make her narrative better? Go ahead and make them for her.

Apply It

▶ On a separate sheet of paper, write your draft. Use the notes you made on pages 43 and 44. Do not worry about spelling and grammar right now. Focus on drafting a clear, interesting story.

▶ After you have written the draft, read it. Then revise it. Use the checklist on page 35 and the one below, which focuses on key elements of a personal narrative.

▶ When you have revised your draft, proofread it to find and fix any mistakes in spelling, capitalization, punctuation, and grammar. Use the checklist on page 36 and the one below.

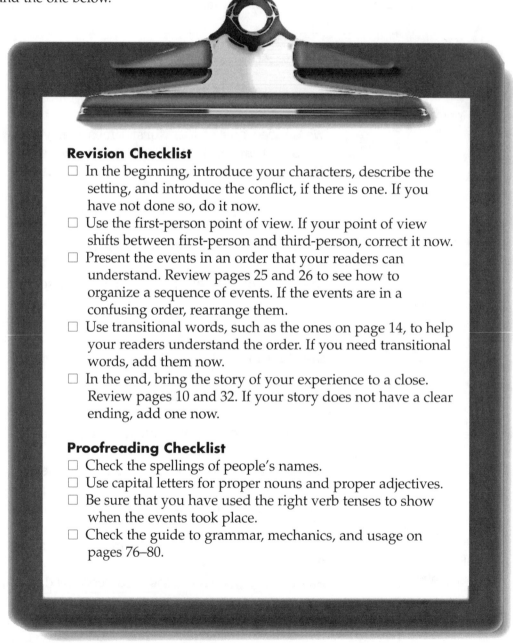

Revision Checklist
☐ In the beginning, introduce your characters, describe the setting, and introduce the conflict, if there is one. If you have not done so, do it now.
☐ Use the first-person point of view. If your point of view shifts between first-person and third-person, correct it now.
☐ Present the events in an order that your readers can understand. Review pages 25 and 26 to see how to organize a sequence of events. If the events are in a confusing order, rearrange them.
☐ Use transitional words, such as the ones on page 14, to help your readers understand the order. If you need transitional words, add them now.
☐ In the end, bring the story of your experience to a close. Review pages 10 and 32. If your story does not have a clear ending, add one now.

Proofreading Checklist
☐ Check the spellings of people's names.
☐ Use capital letters for proper nouns and proper adjectives.
☐ Be sure that you have used the right verb tenses to show when the events took place.
☐ Check the guide to grammar, mechanics, and usage on pages 76–80.

▶ If you can, revise and proofread with a partner. Use the checklists to think of ways to improve your narratives. Listen to your partner's suggestions.

▶ Make a clean copy of your personal narrative. Send it to the school newspaper or literary magazine for publication. Or, work with a group of classmates to put together a class collection of personal narratives.

CHAPTER 2 Writing an Eyewitness Account

In an eyewitness account, you tell what you saw. Have you ever experienced a power blackout? Have you ever attended a student council meeting? What happened? These are examples of firsthand experiences that make good topics for an eyewitness account.

What to Do

Notice what is unique about an eyewitness account. It recreates an event. The details you use to describe the event should be so clear and strong that your audience feels as if they have experienced it, too.

How to Do It

Here is an eyewitness account that a student named Derrick wrote for his school newspaper. Derrick had a chance to spend a day with a reporter for a Los Angeles paper. During the day, he witnessed a fire.

Derrick began with a sentence that hooks the reader's attention.

He told his story in the first-person, but he focused on the events, not on himself.

He organized the account chronologically.

He presented facts in an objective way.

He included details to make the audience feel that they were witnessing the event.

He included an ending that commented on the importance of the event.

> Flames shot from the roof of the apartment building. A strong wind fed the fire. When we arrived on the scene, firefighters were aiming gigantic water hoses at the upper floors. The intense heat kept them well back from the burning building.
>
> As soon as he was out of the car, Aaron Loeb, top reporter for the Monitor, flipped open a notebook and jotted notes. Then he ran over to the fire chief, who was shouting orders to one of his captains.
>
> "Do you know what started the blaze?" Mr. Loeb asked.
>
> "We're not sure yet," said the chief, shaking his head, "but arson is suspected."
>
> "Can I quote you on that?"
>
> The chief gave Mr. Loeb a grim nod and quickly walked away.
>
> Mr. Loeb began running for his car. "I have to get back to the newsroom and write up the story," he shouted. "My deadline is in twenty minutes!"
>
> The fire burned on. The people on the sidewalk, now homeless, would be able to read all about it in the morning paper.

Review It

1. Underline the sentence that tells what was happening when Derrick first got to the fire.
2. Underline two sentences that give details about the fire.
3. Underline the sentences that show the importance of the event.

Lesson 1   Selecting Vivid Details

Vivid details are key elements in an eyewitness account. They help your readers picture what you are telling them. When your details are clear and sharp, then your audience will feel as if they are witnessing the event, too.

What to Do
Use vivid details. Here are three characteristics of a vivid detail:
- It is specific, not general.
- It appeals to at least one of the five senses.
- It is complete. No important piece of information is missing.

How to Do It
Look at the details listed below. The details in the left column are not vivid. They are general, do not appeal to the senses, and do not give full information. The details in the right column are specific, sensory, and complete.

Vague	Vivid
hat	red stocking cap
athlete	seven-foot-tall basketball player
shoes	worn leather sneakers
building	brick warehouse
newspaper	*Los Angeles Monitor*

Review It
▶ Revise the following paragraph from an eyewitness account. Replace the underlined details with more vivid ones. Make your changes right on the page.

The <u>doors</u> flew open and <u>the famous athlete</u> walked toward us. <u>Fans</u> pressed against the fence and screamed. He <u>smiled</u>. I was surrounded by <u>fans</u>, but hoped that he would notice me. I had <u>traveled a long distance</u> to see him.

Apply It
▶ Choose a topic for your eyewitness account. It can be an event that you have already witnessed. In your notebook, jot down details about the event. Remember to make your details vivid.

Lesson 2 Organizing by Chronological Order

Chronological order means that events and details are arranged in the order in which they occur. Transitional words, such as *first*, *next*, *last*, and *finally*, show chronological order. This type of order is usually used in an eyewitness account.

What to Do
When you use chronological order, be sure that your sequence of events is clear. One good way to organize your sequence of events is to use a chain of events chart.

How to Do It
Look at this example. Here is part of a chain of events chart that Derrick made for his eyewitness account of the fire. He arranged his notes as a chain of events to help him organize them. Each event in the chain will become a part of Derrick's eyewitness account.

> **EVENT:** Mr. Loeb and I arrive at the scene of the fire.
> **TIME:** Monday—8:15 a. m.
> **NOTES:** burning building, firefighters aiming water hoses at upper floors, intense heat

> **EVENT:** Mr. Loeb interviews the fire chief.
> **TIME:** Monday—8: 35 a. m.
> **NOTES:** jumps out of the car, flips open notebook, jots notes, runs over to fire chief, shouting orders

> **EVENT:** Mr. Loeb rushes off to write story.
> **TIME:** Monday—9:10 a. m.
> **NOTES:** twenty minutes to write story; title— "Suspicious Fire on West Side"

Review It
▶ Notice how Derrick used chronological order to organize the information in his eyewitness account. He used transitional words and phrases to show the sequence of events. Underline the transitional words and phrases in the account.

> When we arrived on the scene, firefighters were aiming gigantic water hoses at the upper floors. The intense heat kept them well back from the burning building.
> As soon as he was out of the car, Aaron Loeb, top reporter for the <u>Monitor</u> flipped open a notebook and jotted notes. Then he ran over to the fire chief, who was shouting orders to one of his captains.

Apply It

▶ Use this chain of events chart to organize the events of your eyewitness account. Jot down dates, times, notes, and details on the chain of events chart.

START

EVENT: **TIME:** **NOTES:**

↓

EVENT: **TIME:** **NOTES:**

↓

EVENT: **TIME:** **NOTES:**

↓

EVENT: **TIME:** **NOTES:**

↓

EVENT: **TIME:** **NOTES:**

FINISH

Lesson 3 Drafting Your Eyewitness Account

Now you are ready to write the draft of your own eyewitness account. In the drafting stage, the point is to get your words on paper. Focus on *what* you want to say. You can improve the *way* you say it later.

What to Do   Give your eyewitness account an introduction, a body, and a conclusion.

How to Do It   You can begin at the beginning and work right through the draft. This is one way to write a draft. If it doesn't work for you, start somewhere else. Many writers like to start with the body. They write the introduction later.

Draft the Introduction
☐ Begin your eyewitness account with a startling detail that will catch your readers' attention. (For example: "Flames shot from the roof of the apartment building.")
   ▪ Look back over your notes on vivid details from Lesson 1.
   ▪ Which detail stands out? Circle it.
   ▪ Turn it into an attention-grabbing opening statement.
☐ Tell your readers where and when the event took place.
☐ Include yourself in the account as the first-person narrator. Focus on the event, not on yourself.

Draft the Body
☐ Present the sequence of events that you witnessed.
   ▪ Look over your chain of events chart.
   ▪ Write about the events in the order in which they are listed.
   ▪ Begin a new paragraph for each event on your chart. (If you include dialogue, remember to start a new paragraph each time the speaker changes, too.)
   ▪ Be sure that you use vivid details to bring the events to life for your readers. If you don't think your details are vivid enough, use them as they are for now. You can always improve them later.

Draft the Conclusion
☐ Finish with the last event.
☐ Write a response to what you witnessed.
   ▪ Think about what the whole experience meant to you. Write a sentence about that.
   ▪ Think about what it meant to other people. Write a sentence about that.

Apply It   ▶ On a separate sheet of paper, draft your eyewitness account, using the notes and plans you have made. Do not worry about spelling and grammar right now. Get your ideas down on paper.

Lesson 4 Completing Your Eyewitness Account

Remember that an eyewitness account should make your audience feel that they are at the scene of the action. As you revise, pay close attention to how well you have brought the event to life.

What to Do

After you have written the draft, read it. Then revise it. When you have revised your draft, proofread it to find and fix any mistakes in spelling, capitalization, punctuation, and grammar.

How to Do It

Use the revision checklist on page 35 and the one below, which focuses on key elements of an eyewitness account.

- ☐ Open with a statement that will grab your readers' attention. If you have not done that, add a detail now or move one to the beginning.
- ☐ Use vivid details. Make your details more specific, sensory, and complete.
- ☐ Tell your account from the first-person point of view. If you have not, change the point of view now.
- ☐ Use transitional words to show chronological order. If you have not, add them now.
- ☐ Explain the importance of the event. If you have not, add a sentence now.

Use the proofreading checklist on page 36 as you proofread your eyewitness account.

Look at the changes Derrick made when he revised part of his work.

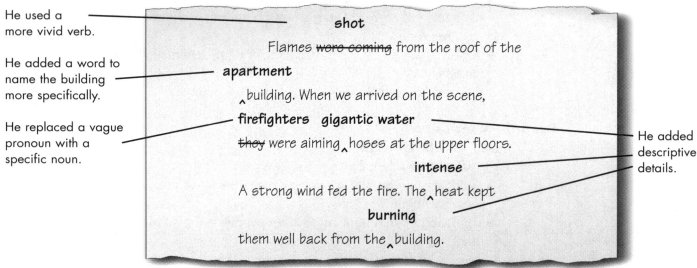

He used a more vivid verb.

He added a word to name the building more specifically.

He replaced a vague pronoun with a specific noun.

He added descriptive details.

> **shot**
> Flames ~~were coming~~ from the roof of the
> **apartment**
> ‸building. When we arrived on the scene,
> **firefighters   gigantic water**
> ~~they~~ were aiming‸hoses at the upper floors.
> **intense**
> A strong wind fed the fire. The‸heat kept
> **burning**
> them well back from the‸building.

Apply It

▶ If you can, revise and proofread with a partner. Suggest ways to improve each other's work and correct errors. Finally, when you are satisfied that your eyewitness account is the best it can be, make a clean copy. Choose one of the following options for publishing your account.
- ■ Read your account aloud to a small group of classmates.
- ■ Submit your account to the school newspaper.

CHAPTER 3 Writing a Humorous Anecdote

Have you heard the story about the dog named Chester? He was a pretty normal dog, except that he only barked at rabbits—Volkswagen Rabbits. Brief stories are called anecdotes. If they are brief and funny, they are called humorous anecdotes.

What to Do

Learn what is unique about a humorous anecdote. It is a short, entertaining account. Usually, a humorous anecdote is about a particular event or episode. It also is often about real people. The purpose of a humorous anecdote is to make your readers laugh. Look at the key elements. A humorous anecdote:

- is brief.
- entertains readers.
- is often about real people.
- usually uses dialogue.
- may make a point or reveal a personality trait.

How to Do It

Look at this humorous anecdote that a student named Jesse wrote.

The anecdote is about real people and a real episode.

The anecdote is brief and entertaining.

Uncle Eli's ridiculous decision is told with a serious tone.

> How long does a big-league pitcher's throwing arm have to be? Once, my brother Franklin and I had a big argument about that question. Franklin claimed that a pitcher's arm had to be longer than normal in order to throw a ball with top speed. I didn't believe him. I said, "It's strength, not length."
>
> My brother yelled, "You're wrong! Big-league pitchers have longer arms than normal people."
>
> We decided to ask the opinion of our Uncle Eli, who is a wise and worldly man. He heard our arguments and scratched his chin. After thinking for a few moments, Uncle Eli answered, "Well, I think a big-league pitcher needs a throwing arm that reaches all the way from his shoulder to his hand."

Review It

1. Circle the names of the people in Jesse's humorous anecdote.
2. Underline examples of dialogue.
3. What does Uncle Eli's answer reveal about his personality?

Lesson 1 Building to the Punch Line

All humorous anecdotes build to the punch line. The punch line is the sentence that makes the point of the anecdote.

What to Do Build a series of events that leads to the punch line. A good tool to help you organize those events and build to the punch line is an event map.

How to Do It Look at this example. It is the event map that Jesse wrote to build toward the punch line of his humorous anecdote.

Event 1

> Franklin and I disagree about the length of a pitcher's arm.

Event 2

> Franklin and I each state our sides of the argument.

Event 3

> We ask Uncle Eli for his opinion.

Punch Line

> Uncle Eli gives us an unexpected opinion.

Review It

1. What does a humorous anecdote build toward?

_____

_____

2. Which event leads to all of the other events in Jesse's plot map?

_____

_____

3. What point does Jesse's punch line make?

_____

_____

Apply It

▶ Use this event map to build toward the punch line of your humorous anecdote. Write a sentence describing each event. Add more boxes if you need them. Then write the punch line for your anecdote.

EVENT 1
This event should introduce the idea or situation that will eventually lead to the punch line.

EVENT 2
This event should bring the reader closer to the punch line.

EVENT 3
This event should set the reader up for the punch line. It should lead right into the punch line.

PUNCH LINE
This is the payoff for the reader, the "joke."

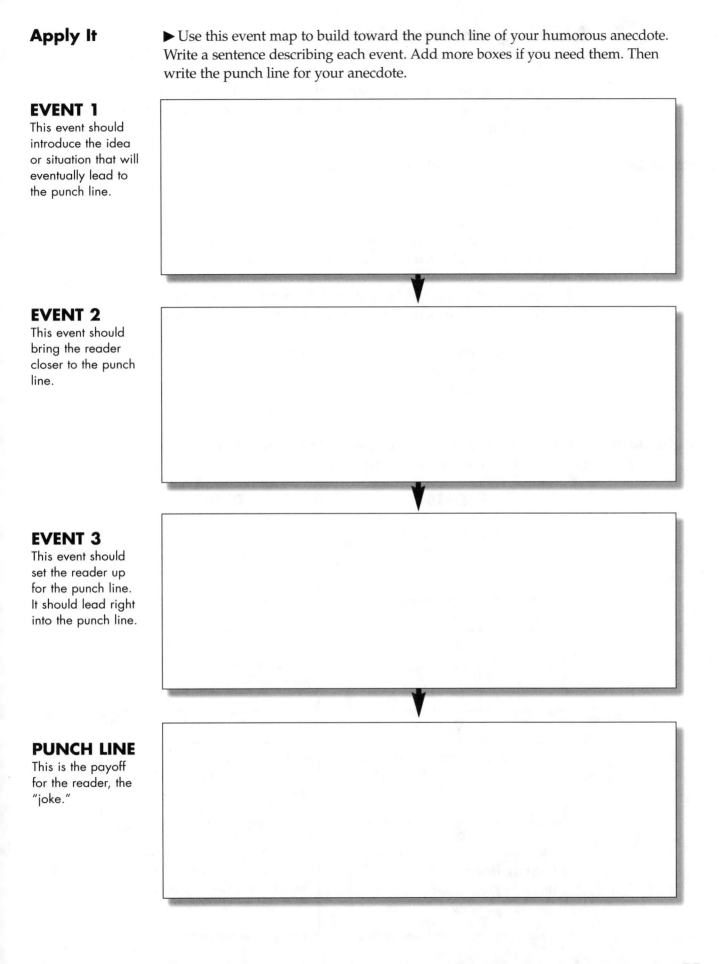

Lesson 2 Making an Anecdote Funny

Because an anecdote is brief, the details in it need to be clear and specific. These clear details will help your readers appreciate the real people and the event you are writing about in your humorous anecdote.

What to Do Use specific details to make an anecdote funny. There are many ways to make an anecdote funny.

- Exaggerate wildly.
- Give an unexpected twist.
- Include unexpected details about a setting or character.
- Tell about a ridiculous situation in a serious tone.

What makes a detail specific? Look at the following list of words and phrases that Jesse changed from general to specific in his humorous anecdote.

General	Specific
two brothers	Franklin and I
a relative	Uncle Eli
pitcher	big-league pitcher

How to Do It A detail map can help you gather specific details about the events in your humorous anecdote. Look at the chart that Jesse created for his anecdote.

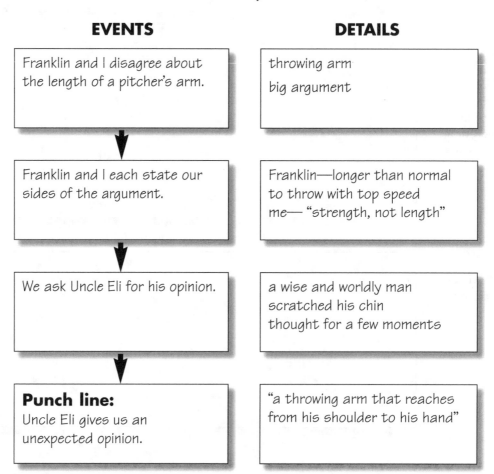

EVENTS

Franklin and I disagree about the length of a pitcher's arm.

↓

Franklin and I each state our sides of the argument.

↓

We ask Uncle Eli for his opinion.

↓

Punch line:
Uncle Eli gives us an unexpected opinion.

DETAILS

throwing arm
big argument

Franklin—longer than normal to throw with top speed
me— "strength, not length"

a wise and worldly man
scratched his chin
thought for a few moments

"a throwing arm that reaches from his shoulder to his hand"

Apply It   ▶ Use this detail map to gather specific details about the events in your anecdote. Next to each event, write the specific details. Then identify your humorous punch line. It may be a wild exaggeration, an unexpected twist, unexpected details, or something ridiculous told in a serious tone.

EVENTS

DETAILS

Punch line:

Lesson 3   Drafting Your Humorous Anecdote

Now you are ready to draft your own humorous anecdote. Remember that everything in the anecdote should build toward the punch line.

What to Do

Use the notes you have made to write the draft of your anecdote.

How to Do It

Follow this checklist to write a draft of your anecdote.

To draft the introduction, use your notes from pages 55 and 57 and:

☐ Start with a sentence that will catch your readers' interest. Use one of the following kinds of opening sentences:

- Ask a question about the punch line. (For example: How long does a big-league pitcher's throwing arm have to be?)
- Make a statement about the punch line, but without giving the punch line away. (For example: A big-league pitcher's throwing arm has to be a special length.)

☐ Introduce the characters who will play parts in the anecdote

☐ Tell about the event that got the action of the anecdote started.

☐ Describe the setting if it is important to the anecdote.

☐ Explain any background information that your audience will need to know to understand the punch line.

To draft the body, use your notes from pages 55 and 57 and:

☐ Write the events in the order that you listed them on page 55.

☐ Begin a new paragraph for each new event.

☐ Begin a new paragraph for each new speaker's dialogue, too.

☐ Add details to bring the events to life and make the anecdote funny. You can use one or more of the following ways to make an anecdote funny:

- Exaggerate wildly.
- Give an unexpected twist.
- Include unexpected details about a setting or character.
- Tell about a ridiculous situation in a serious tone.

To draft the conclusion, use your notes from pages 55 and 57 and:

☐ End with the punch line.

☐ Use details to make the punch line funny. Look again at the checklist for the body of the anecdote.

☐ Do not add anything after the punch line.

Apply It

▶ Use the checklist to draft your humorous anecdote. As you complete each part, place a check mark in the box.

Lesson 4 Completing Your Humorous Anecdote

Now for the final step. Complete your anecdote and share it with your audience.

What to Do   After you have written the draft, read it. Then revise it. When you have revised your draft, proofread it to find and fix any mistakes in spelling, capitalization, punctuation, and grammar.

How to Do It   Use the revision checklist on page 35 and the one below, which focuses on key elements of a humorous anecdote. Use the proofreading checklist on page 36.

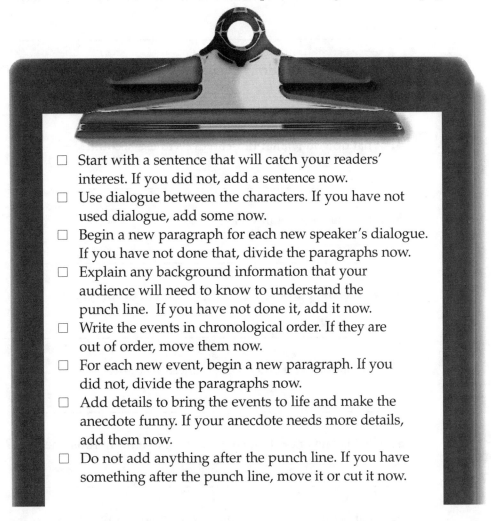

- ☐ Start with a sentence that will catch your readers' interest. If you did not, add a sentence now.
- ☐ Use dialogue between the characters. If you have not used dialogue, add some now.
- ☐ Begin a new paragraph for each new speaker's dialogue. If you have not done that, divide the paragraphs now.
- ☐ Explain any background information that your audience will need to know to understand the punch line. If you have not done it, add it now.
- ☐ Write the events in chronological order. If they are out of order, move them now.
- ☐ For each new event, begin a new paragraph. If you did not, divide the paragraphs now.
- ☐ Add details to bring the events to life and make the anecdote funny. If your anecdote needs more details, add them now.
- ☐ Do not add anything after the punch line. If you have something after the punch line, move it or cut it now.

Apply It   ▶ If you can, revise and proofread with a partner. Read your anecdotes aloud. Suggest ways to improve each other's anecdotes and correct errors.

▶ After you have revised and proofread your anecdote, make the final copy and publish it. Choose one of the following options for publishing your anecdote.
- ■ Read your anecdote to a group of classmates.
- ■ Perform your anecdote with a group of classmates, using gestures and dialogue. Have classmates take the parts of characters in the anecdote.
- ■ Work with classmates to put together a class collection of humorous anecdotes.
- ■ Send your anecdote to the editor of your favorite humor magazine.

What Have You Learned in Unit 3?

Use these questions to gather and review your thoughts about the writing you did in Unit 3. Don't worry about writing complete sentences. Just put some thoughts, ideas, and reactions down for each question.

Personal Narrative

1. Who is the narrator of a personal narrative?

_____

2. How can you gather details about events in a personal narrative?

_____

3. What should you do in the conclusion of a personal narrative?

_____

Eyewitness Account

4. What do you tell about in an eyewitness account?

_____

5. What makes a detail vivid?

_____

6. What is the purpose for using a chain of events chart?

_____

7. How should you end an eyewitness account?

_____

Humorous Anecdote

8. What is one important characteristic of a humorous anecdote?

_____

9. What is one way of making an anecdote funny?

_____

10. What should be the very last element of a humorous anecdote?

_____

▶ If you can, share your answers with a partner or group. Share the ideas and experiences you had. Talk about problems you had while writing. Talk about your successes, too. Develop a group list of tips for each kind of writing you did in this unit.

UNIT 4 Writing on Assignment

Sometimes, you will be told what to write. You will be given an assignment. This is true of adult writers, too. In all types of careers, people have writing to do as part of their jobs. Often, their writing assignments have deadlines. A deadline is the time when a writing project must be completed. To meet a deadline, you may have to shorten some of the writing steps.

What to Do

Become familiar with the two different kinds of narration that you will write in this unit:

    A Test Essay
    A Biographical Account

How to Do It

Learn the key elements of each kind of narration that you will write.

A test essay is unique in two important ways.

First, it is written in response to a question or a set of directions. You have to make sure that you answer the question or follow the directions.

Second, a test essay is written under a deadline. You must work quickly and efficiently. You must organize your thoughts as quickly as possible. You must limit your answer to what you can write before the deadline. You will not have much time to revise. You will be able to make only the most important changes.

A biographical account has one main purpose: to capture part of a person's life in words.

A biographical account creates a vivid portrait of a real person whom the writer finds interesting. It includes a physical description, observations about the person's personality, and biographical information. It also reveals how you, the writer, feel toward the subject.

Apply It

▶ Find examples of each of the types of narration you will write in this unit. Look for biographical accounts in magazines. Look for an essay you have written for a test. If you can, work with a group to discuss how the writers of the examples (including you) have told their stories. Save the examples in your notebook.

CHAPTER 1 Writing a Test Essay

Many tests in English and social studies classes include essays. Often, a test will ask you to read a statement and then write a narrative essay in which you tell the story of something that happened. Your teacher will expect you to put events in order and include important details. You can do well on essay tests by understanding essay test questions and organizing your answers.

What to Do

Learn what is unique about a test essay. A test essay is a short piece of writing that tells what you know about a topic. This type of essay follows the standard format of all narrative essays. It has a beginning, middle, and end. However, a test essay is unique. Most often, it is written in response to a prompt. A prompt is a question or a set of directions. Here is a sample test prompt.

> The Constitution describes how our government is organized. Tell the story of how the Constitution was written. Include the major people involved. Follow the events from the time when the Constitutional Convention began to the time when the Constitution was signed.

How to Do It

Study this example. It is part of an essay that a student named Taro wrote in response to the prompt.

BEGINNING
The beginning restates the main goal of the prompt. It begins the story at the point where the prompt said to begin. It gives specific dates. It names the important people in the story.

> The story of the writing of the Constitution is the story of a compromise. In the summer of 1787, a group of 55 men from 12 states met in Philadelphia. The men included Edmund Randolph, Benjamin Franklin, George Washington, and Alexander Hamilton. At the meeting, the men decided to create a new government.

MIDDLE
The middle tells the events in the story in order. It includes transitions that make the timing of events clear.

> First, Edmund Randolph presented what came to be called the Virginia Plan. It was written by James Madison. In the Virginia Plan, large states had more votes than smaller states.
>
> Next, William Paterson presented what came to be called the New Jersey Plan. It described a government in which large states and smaller states had equal votes.

Review It

▶ Answer the following questions about the answer that Taro wrote.

1. What is the first event mentioned in Taro's test essay?

_____

2. When did it take place?

_____

3. Underline the transitional word that Taro used to start the second paragraph.

▶ Read the rest of Taro's test essay. Then follow the directions below it.

> For a while, the delegates could not agree. Supporters of the Virginia Plan opposed the New Jersey Plan.
>
> Finally, the delegates agreed to a plan called the Connecticut Compromise. In this plan, the new Congress would have two houses. In one house, each state would have one vote. In the other, each state would have a number of votes based on its population.
>
> By September, the delegates had written their final plan for the new government. On September 17, 1787, the plans and compromises finally ended. The Constitution was signed.

▶ On the lines below, list the events that Taro mentioned in each of his paragraphs.

4. In the paragraph beginning "For a while," the event is:

_____

5. In the paragraph beginning "Finally," the event is:

_____

6. In the paragraph beginning "By September," the event is:

_____

Lesson 1   Understanding the Prompt

Most test essays have to be planned and written quickly. You have only a certain amount of time before the test period is over. Therefore, you must organize your thoughts as quickly as possible.

What to Do

The first step in writing a great test essay is to focus on the prompt. Decide exactly what it asks you to do or tells you to do. Those are your reasons for writing.

How to Do It

Study the prompt from Taro's essay test as an example. Note the key words that Taro underlined.

> The Constitution describes how our government is organized. <u>Tell the story of how the Constitution was written.</u> <u>Include the major people</u> involved. Follow the events <u>from the time when the Constitutional Convention began to the time when the Constitution was signed.</u>

Taro analyzed the prompt to understand the assignment. He found the key words *tell, include, from,* and *to.* These key words toled him to do four things:

1. Tell the story of the writing of the Constitution.
2. Tell who was involved.
3. Start with the Constitutional Convention.
4. End with the signing of the Constitution.

Apply It

▶ Read this prompt. Underline key words and phrases that tell what the purpose for writing is.

> The civil rights movement grew rapidly after the Montgomery, Alabama, bus boycott. Trace the history of the bus boycott. Include the key figures. Begin your account with Rosa Parks's refusal to give up her seat. Finish with the desegregation of the buses.

Lesson 2 Organizing Your Thoughts Quickly

When you answer a test prompt, you must limit your answer to what you can cover in a few paragraphs. You do not have much time, so you have to get organized quickly.

What to Do The body of a narrative test essay should be organized in chronological order. An outline can help you put events in order.

How to Do It Here is the brief outline that Taro used when planning his test essay about the Constitution. He put the events in the order in which they happened.

I. Meeting in Philadelphia
   A. summer of 1787
   B. Edmund Randolph, Benjamin Franklin, George Washington, Alexander Hamilton, William Paterson
II. First Plan—the Virginia Plan
   A. Edmund Randolph presented
   B. large states had more votes
III. Second Plan—the New Jersey Plan
   A. William Paterson presented
   B. large states and smaller states had equal votes
IV. Third Plan—the Connecticut Compromise
   A. new Congress would have two houses
   B. used both methods of allotting votes
V. The final version
   A. signed September 17, 1787
   B. result of plans and compromises

Apply It ▶ Look at the test prompt that you analyzed on the bottom of page 64. Find information about it in your social studies book or in an encyclopedia. If you cannot find information about that prompt, use the following as a test prompt.

Your school career is part of your personal history. In five paragraphs, tell the story of your school career. Include the major people involved. Follow the events from your first day in school to an outstanding event this year.

▶ In the outline below, quickly jot down notes to organize ideas for an answer to the prompt you have chosen. Give yourself a time limit of 5 to 10 minutes.

FIRST EVENT I. _____

    DETAIL   A. _____

    DETAIL   B. _____

NEXT EVENT II. _____

    DETAIL   A. _____

    DETAIL   B. _____

NEXT EVENT III _____

    DETAIL   A. _____

    DETAIL   B. _____

NEXT EVENT IV _____

    DETAIL   A. _____

    DETAIL   B. _____

LAST EVENT V. _____

    DETAIL   A. _____

    DETAIL   B. _____

Lesson 3 Drafting Under a Deadline

A deadline is a writer's term for the date or time when a writing project must be completed. To meet a deadline, you may have to shorten some of the writing steps.

What to Do

Adjust to the deadline. You may have only thirty minutes to an hour to complete your essay. Therefore, you must work as quickly and efficiently as possible.

How to Do It

These tips will help you to get organized and draft your narrative test essay.

Organizing

- Quickly make an outline. Look it over. Make sure that it is clear and complete.
- Be sure that the events are listed in the order in which you will present them. If the order is not right, cross out the numbers and renumber your outline.

Drafting

- Do not let the time pressure get to you. Relax. You have analyzed the prompt and made complete notes. The most difficult part of the writing assignment is actually over.
- Write or print as neatly as possible. Because this is a test, you probably will not be able to make a fresh final copy of your essay.
- Skip a line between lines of writing. These blank lines will leave you space to make revisions and proofreading corrections once your draft is complete.
- Follow these steps to complete your draft quickly. Refer to your outline as you write.
  - **Introduction**
    Begin with a sentence that tells what story will follow.
    Meet any requirements of the prompt that may not come up in the rest of the essay. For example: "Mention the major people involved."
  - **Body**
    Include all the events on your outline. Start a new paragraph for each event.
  - **Conclusion**
    End with a sentence that tells what story your reader has just read.

Apply It

▶ Now you are ready to write your own test essay. On a separate sheet of paper, write a complete draft of your test essay. Use the outline you made on page 66. If you wish, set a time limit for yourself so that you can practice writing under a deadline. Allow yourself thirty minutes in total to answer the question. Spend 5 to 10 minutes planning and organizing. Spend about 15 minutes writing the draft. That should leave you 5 to 10 minutes to revise and proofread in Lesson 4.

Lesson 4   Completing a Test Essay

When you are working under a deadline, you will not have time to make all the changes you would like to make. Make the most important ones first. Those are the ones that affect the meaning of your work.

What to Do

Finish the draft of your essay before your time is up. You want to have enough time left in the test period to go over it quickly.

How to Do It

Because you are taking a test, you will not be able to revise and proofread with a partner. Make any changes that you feel will improve your test essay. Write or print as neatly as possible, and make it clear where words and phrases should be inserted. Rely on your own good judgment. These hints will help.

- Be sure that you have done everything that the prompt asks you to do. If you have overlooked anything, add it now.
- Be sure that no important events are missing. Add any that are missing.
- Check the spellings of words. If you are not sure of one, use another word that you can spell.
- Check for incomplete sentences. Give each sentence the subject or verb that it needs.

Look at the changes Taro made when he revised and proofread the beginning of his test essay.

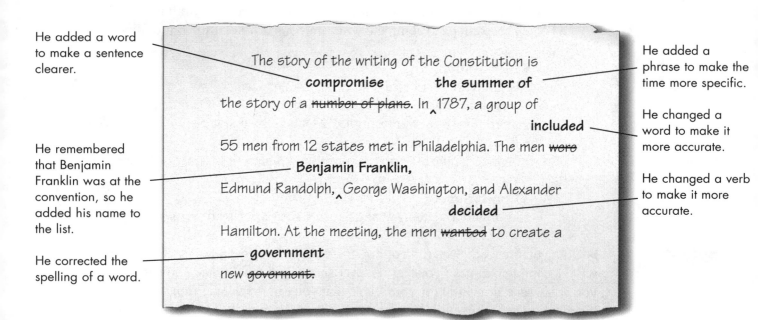

He added a word to make a sentence clearer.

He added a phrase to make the time more specific.

He changed a word to make it more accurate.

He remembered that Benjamin Franklin was at the convention, so he added his name to the list.

He changed a verb to make it more accurate.

He corrected the spelling of a word.

The story of the writing of the Constitution is ~~compromise~~ **the summer of** the story of a ~~number of plans~~. In 1787, a group of **included** 55 men from 12 states met in Philadelphia. The men ~~were~~ **Benjamin Franklin,** Edmund Randolph, George Washington, and Alexander **decided** Hamilton. At the meeting, the men ~~wanted~~ to create a **government** new ~~goverment~~.

Apply It

▶ Revise and proofread the draft of your test essay. Work right on the draft. Make the changes as neatly as you can.

CHAPTER 2 Writing a Biographical Account

Whom do you admire? Do you think one of your relatives leads an interesting life? What about your favorite teacher or neighbor? During this special project, you will learn about the life of someone by writing a biographical account.

What to Do

Learn the key elements of a biographical account:
- It creates a vivid portrait of a real person.
- It focuses on someone who interests you.
- It tells a story of the person's life.
- It reveals how you feel about the person.

How to Do It

Look at this example. It is a biographical account that a student named Rico wrote. Rico wrote his account in three parts—a beginning, middle, and end.

BEGINNING
Rico introduced his subject by telling what he is like now.

MIDDLE
Rico told his grandfather's story in chronological order. He used transitional words and phrases to show when events happened.

END
Rico brought the story up to the present time. He finished by again showing what his grandfather is like now.

> My grandfather does not live in a house. He does not have a backyard, yet he grows the most beautiful garden I have ever seen. On the rooftop of our apartment, he grows a garden of peppers, tomatillos, cilantro, onions, and corn.
>
> Born in Jalisco, Mexico, my grandfather came to the United States when he was twelve. He learned about gardening from his parents, who grew all their own food.
>
> Ten years ago, he began the rooftop garden. Now he is known throughout our neighborhood as "the gardener." Each spring, neighbors place vegetable orders with him.
>
> On any day in spring and summer he can be found working in his rooftop garden. "Taking care of a garden is good for the hands and good for the heart," he says.
>
> On Saturdays, neighborhood kids help him with the garden. "Maybe they'll all grow up to be gardeners," he says. "Imagine a city with thousands of rooftop gardens!"

Apply It

▶ Choose someone interesting to write about. This person will be the "subject" of your biographical account. Your subject must be living and must agree to be interviewed. What do you want to tell people about your subject? In your notebook, jot down ideas.

Lesson 1 Getting Information from an Interview

An interview is a process of gathering information on a topic by asking a person questions.

What to Do Prepare for an interview with your subject. Write down the questions you want to ask your subject. Here are a few hints for planning your interview questions.
- Keep your purpose in mind.
- Avoid questions that can be answered "yes" or "no."
- Start questions with the words *who, what, why, when, where,* and *how.*
- List your questions in a logical order.
- Because you will be writing a story, be sure to ask questions that will help you put the events in chronological order.
- Leave space after each question to write the answer.

How to Do It Here are the questions Rico wrote for the interview with his grandfather.

Where were you born?

When did you come to the United States?

Who taught you how to grow a garden?

When did that happen?

When did you begin the rooftop garden?

What do you grow in your garden?

When do you work in your garden?

What do you like most about gardening?

Why do you let the neighborhood kids help you?

How has a garden made a difference in your life?

Review It ▶ Underline the questions that will help Rico put events in chronological order.

Apply It ▶ On a separate sheet of paper, write down the interview questions you want to ask your subject. Explain the writing project to your subject, and set up an interview time. During the interview take notes and write the answers to your questions.

Lesson 2 Organizing from an Angle

In the notes from your interview, you will probably find details and quotations. You may also find anecdotes,or short stories, that your subject told you. These notes reveal the personality of your subject. You have to organize them into a story for your readers.

What to Do It
You can organize your biographical account in four different ways. Here are a few hints about each type of organization.
- Important Events
  Tell about events in your subject's life that affected what he or she is today.
- Typical Day
  Tell about a typical day in the life of your subject.
- Personality Traits
  Tell anecdotes about your subject that reveal his or her personality.
- Road to Discovery
  Tell how you tried to learn about your subject and what you discovered.

How to Do It
Rico used the "Important Events" organization for the biographical account that you saw on page 69. He also thought about using the "Typical Day" method of organization. Look at his notes for that:

A Typical Day in the Life of My Grandfather
- He gets up at 5:30 every morning.
- After eating breakfast, he climbs the stairs to the roof.
- He inspects the plants for slugs and other bugs.
- He waters the garden before lunch.
- He eats lunch with my grandmother.
- After lunch, he takes a nap.
- He neatens the straw paths between the garden beds.
- He picks ripe tomatoes for homemade salsa.
- He sits on the rooftop with my grandmother and me.
- I help him weed a few rows of the garden.
- We talk about the day until dinner time.
- We climb down the stairs back to the apartment.

Review It
▶ Underline the words and phrases that tell when events happen.

Apply It ▶ Choose a method of organization for your biographical account. Use the following chart to map it out. On the left, list the events that you plan to use. On the right, add details, anecdotes, and quotations from the answers your subject gave during the interview. Write these items in the boxes.

EVENTS **DETAILS**

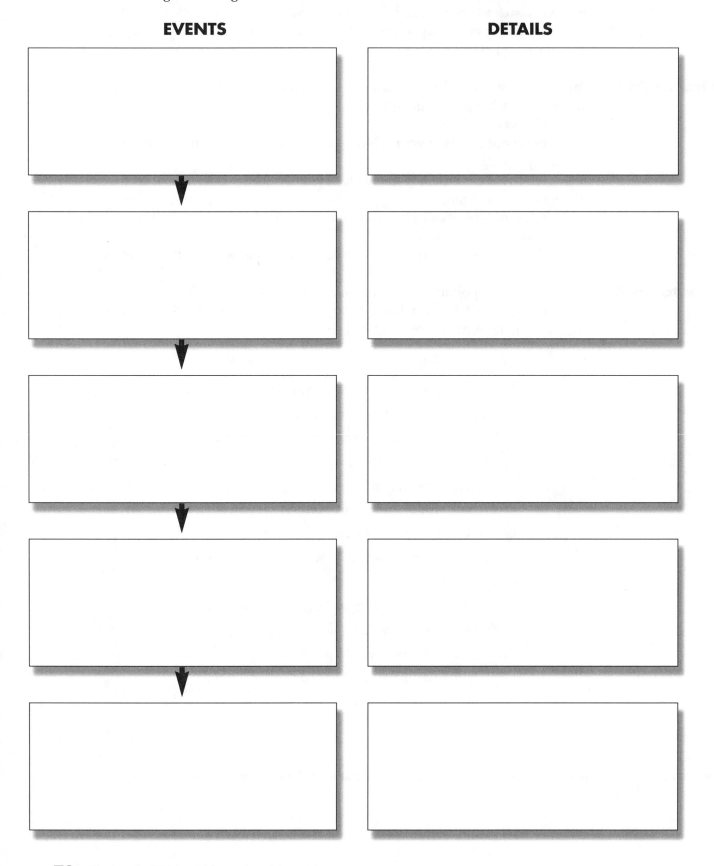

Lesson 3 Writing Your Biographical Account

Now you are ready to write your own biographical account.

What to Do Use your notes to write the draft of your biographical account.

How to Do It Use the notes you took during your interview and organized on page 72. Do not worry about spelling and grammar right now. Focus on drafting your subject's story. Here are hints for writing the draft:

Introduction
- Begin by telling what your subject is like now.
- Include a quotation from your subject if you have one that fits here.

Body
- Tell your subject's story in chronological order.
- Use transitional words and phrases to tell your readers when events happened.
- Include quotations from your subject if you have any that fit here.

Conclusion
- Finish by returning to your subject in the present.
- Include a quotation from your subject if you have one that fits here.

After you have written the draft, read it. Use the checklist on page 35 to help you revise it. When you have revised your draft, proofread it to find and fix any mistakes in spelling, capitalization, punctuation, and grammar. To help you proofread, use the checklist on page 36 and the one below.

Proofreading Checklist
- ☐ Check the spellings of names of people and places.
- ☐ Capitalize proper nouns and proper adjectives.
- ☐ Check the guide to grammar, mechanics, and usage on pages 76–80.

Apply It ▶ On a separate sheet of paper, write your draft. If you can, exchange accounts with a partner. Proofread each other's accounts for spelling, grammar, and punctuation errors. After you have written, revised, and proofread your account, make a clean copy. You may want to make a cover for the account, add photographs or drawings, and present it to your subject.

What Have You Learned in Unit 4?

Use these questions to gather and review your thoughts about the writing you did in Unit 4. Don't worry about writing complete sentences. Just put some thoughts, ideas, and reactions down for each question.

A Test Essay

1. What is a test essay prompt?

_____

2. What should you look for in a test essay prompt?

_____

3. How can you quickly organize your thoughts for a test essay?

_____

4. Why should you stop drafting a few minutes before the deadline?

_____

5. Why is it a good idea to skip a line between lines of writing?

_____

A Biographical Account

6. What is one purpose of a biographical account?

_____

7. What should you try to do in the middle of a biographical account?

_____

8. What is one hint for planning an interview?

_____

9. What is one way of organizing a biographical account?

_____

10. Why did you choose the method of organization that you used for your biographical account?

_____

▶ If you can, share your answers with a partner or group. Talk about the ideas and experiences you had. Share problems and successes you had while writing. Develop a group list of tips for each kind of writing you did in this unit.

The Writing Process

The writing process

What happens when a writer turns words into a story or an essay? He or she follows a set of steps, from start to finish. These steps make up the writing process. If you follow the same steps, you can make the process work for you.

What is a process?

A process is a series of steps that lead to a goal. Each step brings the process closer to the goal. Suppose you wanted to grow a pepper plant in a pot. Growing a plant is a process. You choose seeds, plant them, water the plants, and pull weeds. Each step gets you closer to your goal, and finally you pick the peppers.

What is the writing process?

There are five main steps in the writing process. They are prewriting, drafting, revising, proofreading, and publishing. This chart shows them. You won't always follow them in order, and you may move back and forth between stages.

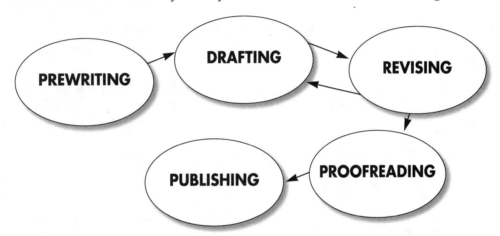

Prewriting

In prewriting, you decide what to write. This step is like deciding what seeds to grow. You explore your idea. You think about it and gather information about it. You organize your ideas. You think about the people you will be writing for. You decide what they need to know and how you want to tell it to them.

Drafting

In drafting, you put your ideas into words. You shape your words into sentences. You build your sentences into paragraphs. As you draft, you do not have to worry about parts that are not quite right. You will fix them in the next stage.

Revising

In revising, you improve your draft. You look for weak spots, such as a word that is not quite right. You make changes, or revisions, to strengthen those spots. Notice that the arrows in the drafting and revising sections can lead you back and forth. This part of the process is like watering and weeding in the growing process.

Proofreading

When you are satisfied with your revised work, you turn to proofreading. This stage is sometimes called editing. In this step, you check for and correct any errors you may have made in grammar, usage, and mechanics, including spelling.

Publishing

Finally, in the publishing stage, you make a final copy and publish it or share it with an audience.

A Guide for Writers: Grammar, Mechanics, and Usage

GRAMMAR

Nouns A **noun** is the name of a person, place, or thing. A **common noun** names any person, place, or thing. A **proper noun** names a particular person, place, or thing.

Common Nouns	Proper Nouns
ballplayer	Cal Ripken
city	Los Angeles
river	Hudson River
country	Peru
street	Jackson Avenue

Pronouns Pronouns are words that stand for or take the place of nouns.
The subject pronouns are:

Singular	Plural
I	we
you	you
he	they
she	they
it	they

Use a **subject pronoun** as the subject of a sentence.

Incorrect
Her and Rosa will be here soon.
Revision
She and Rosa will be here soon.

Use **subject pronouns** after the linking verb *to be*.

Incorrect
The winners were Leroy and him.
Revision
The winners were Leroy and he.

The object pronouns are:

Singular	Plural
me	us
you	you
him	them
her	them
it	them

Use **object pronouns** as the direct objects of sentences. A direct object receives the action in a sentence.

Incorrect
Rosa will call Leo and I.
Revision
Rosa will call Leo and me.

Use object pronouns as objects of prepositions. The object of a preposition is a noun or pronoun at the end of a prepositional phrase. (See **Prepositions**.)

Incorrect
Selena wrote to Duane and I.
Revision
Selena wrote to Duane and me.

Possessive pronouns show ownership. The possessive pronouns are:

Singular	Plural
my	our
your	your
his	their
her	their
its	their

Verbs A **verb** is a word that shows action or the fact that something exists. Verbs change form to show time. These forms are called *tenses*.

Use **irregular verbs** correctly. Some verbs have unusual forms for showing that an action happened in the past. When in doubt, check a dictionary or ask a good editor (such as your teacher).

Incorrect
The group sung their hits.
Revision
The group sang their hits.

Adjectives An **adjective** is a word used to describe a noun or pronoun. A **proper adjective** is made from a proper noun. It names a particular person, place, or thing.

Use the correct form to compare adjectives. To compare two persons, places, or things, use the **comparative** form. Add *-er* to most short adjectives. Use *more* with longer adjectives. Use one or the other, not both.

Incorrect	Revision
more long movie	longer movie
thrillinger movie	more thrilling movie
more newer movie	newer movie

To compare more than two persons, places, or things, use the **superlative** form. Add -*est* to most short adjectives. Use *most* with longer adjectives. Use one or the other, not both.

Incorrect	Revision
most slow bus	slowest bus
comfortablest bus	most comfortable bus
most noisiest bus	noisiest bus

Some adjectives use different words for comparisons.

Examples

bad	worse	worst
good	better	best

Adverbs An **adverb** is a word that modifies a verb, an adjective, or another adverb.

Do not use an adjective when you need an adverb.

Incorrect	Revision
We did the job good.	We did the job well.
We did it quick.	We did it quickly.

Use the correct form to compare adverbs. To compare two actions, use the **comparative form**. Add -*er* to most short adverbs. Use *more* with most adverbs. Use one or the other, not both.

Incorrect	Revision
spoke more softlier	spoke more softly
started more later	started later

To compare more than two actions, use the **superlative form**. 1. Use -*est* with some short adverbs. 2. Use *most* with most adverbs. 3. Use one or the other, not both.

Incorrect	Revision
spoke most softliest	spoke most softly
started most latest	started latest

Some adverbs use different words for comparisons.

Examples

badly	worse	worst
well	better	best

Prepositions A **preposition** is a word that relates the noun or pronoun following it to another word in the sentence.

Examples

in	on	off	of	under
over	along	beside	above	between

I saw the funnel of a tornado in the distance. The funnel was moving in my direction.

Sentences A **sentence** is a group of words with two main parts: a complete subject and a complete predicate. Together these parts express a complete thought.

Use complete sentences, not **fragments**. A complete sentence has a subject and a verb. A fragment is missing one of those parts. Correct a fragment by adding the missing part.

Fragment
The book written by Gary Soto.
Revision
The book was written by Gary Soto.
Fragment
Because the rain finally stopped.
Revision
We went out because the rain finally stopped.

Avoid **run-on sentences**. A run-on sentence is really more than one sentence. Correct a run-on sentence by dividing it into two (or more) sentences.

Run-on
For months I saved all the money I earned, and I never spent any of it, and finally I had enough for the class trip.
Revision
For months I saved all the money I earned. I never spent any of it. Finally I had enough for the class trip.

Subject-Verb Agreement Make the subject and verb of a sentence agree in number. To make a subject and verb agree, make sure that both are **singular** or both are **plural**. A singular subject names one person, place, or thing. A plural subject names more than one person, place, or thing.

Incorrect
Some parts is missing.
Revision
Some parts are missing.

Be careful when a **prepositional phrase** comes between the subject and the verb. The verb must agree with the subject, not with the object of the preposition.

Incorrect
One of the parts are missing.
Revision
One of the parts is missing.

The pronoun *I* is singular, but it nearly always takes the plural form of a verb. (The only exceptions are *am* and *was*, which are singular forms of the verb *to be*.)

Incorrect
I urges you to act now.
Revision
I urge you to act now.
Incorrect
I is nearly ready.
Revision
I am nearly ready.

Phrases A **phrase** is a group of words, without a subject and verb, that works in a sentence as one part of speech.

A **prepositional phrase** is a group of words that includes a **preposition** and the **object of the preposition**, a noun or pronoun. The whole phrase works like an adjective or adverb. It modifies the meaning of another word or group of words.

Keep prepositions and their phrases close to the words they modify. Your sentence may not say what you mean if a prepositional phrase is in the wrong place.

One Meaning
The car with stripes looks great.
(but another car does not)
Another Meaning
The car looks great with stripes.
(but not without stripes)

Negatives A **negative** is a word or word part

that means "not." The word *not* itself is a negative. So are *nobody* and *nowhere*. The contraction *-n't* is made from *not*. When *-n't* is part of a word, it is a negative.

Use only one negative in a sentence. More than one negative in a sentence is a "double negative." Remove double negatives in your sentences.

Incorrect
We don't have no blank cassettes.
Revision
We don't have any blank cassettes.
We have no blank cassettes.

MECHANICS

Capitalization Capitalize the first word of a sentence.

Incorrect
the sun looked like an orange.
Revision
The sun looked like an orange.

Capitalize proper nouns.

Incorrect	**Revision**
boston red sox	Boston Red Sox
ernesto galarza	Ernesto Galarza
thailand	Thailand

Capitalize proper adjectives.

Incorrect
foreign and american cars
Revision
foreign and American cars

Capitalize the first word and all important words in titles of books, movies, and other works of art.

Incorrect	**Revision**
Jurassic park	*Jurassic Park*

Capitalize a person's title when it is followed by the person's name.

Incorrect	**Revision**
senator Marston	Senator Marston

Punctuation

End Marks Use an end mark at the end of

every sentence. Use a period to end a sentence that makes a statement or gives a command. Use a question mark to end a question. Use an exclamation point after a statement showing strong emotion.

Incorrect
This is the movie to see
Have you seen it already
Yes, and it's great

Revisions
This is the movie to see.
Have you seen it already?
Yes, and it's great!

Commas Use a comma between the two independent clauses in a compound sentence.

Incorrect
Levon was standing in the doorway and his brother was sitting on the sofa.

Revision
Levon was standing in the doorway, and his brother was sitting on the sofa.

Use commas to separate three or more words in a series.

Incorrect
I bought a shirt a cap and a compact disc.

Revision
I bought a shirt, a cap, and a compact disc.

Use commas to set the rest of the sentence apart from the spoken words in a direct quotation.

Incorrect
She said "I'm not ready."
"Wait here" he said "until I return."

Revision
She said, "I'm not ready."
"Wait here," he said, "until I return."

Quotation Marks A direct quotation represents a person's exact words. Use quotation marks around the words the speaker says.

Incorrect
Mr. Hsu said, Take tomorrow off.

Revision
Mr. Hsu said, "Take tomorrow off."

When you use a comma or a period with a direct quotation, place it inside the final quotation mark.

Incorrect
"I'll see you tomorrow", I said.
She said, "I'll be waiting".

Revision
"I'll see you tomorrow," I said.
She said, "I'll be waiting."

When you use a question mark or exclamation point with a direct quotation, place it inside the quotation marks if it goes with the speaker's words.

Incorrect
I called, "Is anybody home"?
A voice answered, "I'll be right there"!

Revision
I called, "Is anybody home?"
A voice answered, "I'll be right there!"

Dialogue is written conversation. When you write dialogue, start a new paragraph each time the speaker changes. Begin a new paragraph each time a different person speaks.

Incorrect
"Good morning," he said. "Says who?" I answered.

Revision
"Good morning," he said.
"Says who?" I answered.

Apostrophes A possessive noun shows ownership, as *Luis's* does in *Luis's dog*. To make a singular noun possessive, add an apostrophe (') and an *s*, no matter what letter ends the noun.

Noun	Possessive
student	student's
boss	boss's

To make a plural noun possessive, add an apostrophe and an *s* if the noun ends with some letter other than *s*. Add only an apostrophe if the noun ends with *s*.

Noun	Possessive
children	children's
students	students'
families	families'
lawyers	lawyers'

Possessive pronouns show ownership, like possessive nouns. However, possessive pronouns are not spelled with apostrophes.

Incorrect
Those snapshots are their's.
The dog ate it's food.
Revision
Those snapshots are theirs.
The dog ate its food.

USAGE

bad, badly Use *bad* after linking verbs, such as *feel*, *look*, and *seem*. Use *badly* whenever an adverb is needed.

Incorrect
I felt badly about not being able to play in the game.
Revision
I felt bad about not being able to play in the game.

beside, besides Do not confuse these two prepositions, which have different meanings. Beside means "at the side of" or "close to." Besides means "in addition to."

Incorrect
I wondered whether anyone would be going on the trip beside the usual group.
Revision
I wondered whether anyone would be going on the trip besides the usual group.

can, may The verb *can* generally refers to the ability to do something. The verb *may* generally refers to permission to do something.

Incorrect
"Can I have the last hamburger?" he asked.
Revision
"May I have the last hamburger?" he asked.

good, well Use the predicate adjective *good* after linking verbs, such as *feel*, *look*, *smell*, *taste*, and *seem*. Use *well* whenever you need an adverb.

Incorrect
We hadn't won the game, but we could hold our heads high because we knew that we played good.
Revision
We hadn't won the game, but we could hold our heads high because we knew that we played well.

its, it's Do not confuse the possessive pronoun *its* with the contraction *it's*, standing for *it is* or *it has*.

Incorrect
That dog has something stuck in it's paw.
Revision
That dog has something stuck in its paw.

of, have Do not use *of* in place of *have* after auxiliary verbs, such as *would*, *could*, *should*, *may*, *might*, or *must*.

Incorrect
You should of seen the way Hakeem went up for the rebound.
Revision
You should have seen the way Hakeem went up for the rebound.

than, then The conjunction *than* is used to connect the two parts of a comparison. Do not confuse *than* with the adverb *then*, which usually refers to time.

Incorrect
My brother is exactly a year older then I am.
Revision
My brother is exactly a year older than I am.

their, there, they're Do not confuse the spellings of these three words. *Their* is a possessive pronoun and always modifies a noun. *There* is usually used either at the beginning of a sentence or as an adverb. *They're* is a contraction for *they are*.

Incorrect
"Are those they're sweat pants?" I asked. "No," he said. "There over their, behind the lockers."
Revision
"Are those their sweat pants?" I asked. "No," he said. "They're over there, behind the lockers."